THE BENIGN HUMORISTS

The
Benign Humorists

by
Richard S. Carlson

Archon Books / 1975

Library of Congress Cataloging in Publication Data

Carlson, Richard S   1942-
   The benign humorists.

   Bibliography: p.
   Includes index.
1. English wit and humor—History and criticism. 2. English
literature—19th century—History and criticism. 3. English
literature—20th century—History and criticism. I. Title.
PR937.C37   823'.0876   74-26985
ISBN 0-208-01476-4

PR
931
C37

© 1975 by Richard S. Carlson
First published 1975 as an Archon Book,
an imprint of THE SHOE STRING PRESS, INC.,

For Joshua

Contents

Introduction

In the late nineteenth and early twentieth centuries, a rather small group of writers developed both a literary form and language that remains inventive, congenial and accomplished. Benign humorists Lewis Carroll, Edward Lear, Beatrix Potter, A.A. Milne, P.G. Wodehouse, Kenneth Grahame, and Walter de la Mare prospected and mined a vein of humor quite different from the literature of wit and satire which critically prevailed in nineteenth- and twentieth-century England.

The humorists of the nineteenth and twentieth centuries saw the possibility of a benign literature and they posited their animals and engagingly primitive humans into a literary mayonnaise. Their literature, thick with fuss and fun, continues to beard many critics into addressing more seriously other literatures in the English comic tradition. The literature of the benign humorists has gone relatively unaddressed as many literary scholars, not always inappropriately, have turned their critical energies toward literary satire and wit. Certainly, the critical oversight has been one of omission rather than commission.

In addition to its considerable literary artistry, the literature of the benign humorists continues to provide a rather curious socio-literary service. While William Dean Howells, America's fin de siecle custodian of "genteel traditions," would try to fix, or at least perpetuate, America's "Victorian innocence" by showing its cruel defeat in such novels as *The Rise and Fall of Silas Lapham,* and while England's Aldous Huxley updated and even surrealized science in one book and then thought it a treasure to "spite-on" his friends in the next, the benign humorists were content to merely entertain their reading publics. But after times hardened in the twentieth century, many intellectuals found themselves philosophically tangled and ill-equipped to find literary artistry in any writing that did not catalog a confused people and parched time. As a result, American and English custodians of culture asked for a literature that would speak *for* social groups and *about* common ills. To such theory, however, the benign humorists delivered their no thank yous in a constant output of sportive books spilling with fun. The benign humorists, however, wrote about times past and imaginary eras. Unlike the literary wits and satirists in the nineteenth and early twentieth centuries who felt it incumbent upon themselves to comment on the problems and changing institutions of the new century, the humorists refused to deal with cultural and societal considerations.

While the American sense of humor denied the attractions of an innocent benign humor, thereby enabling comic wit to rule the American comic tradition, such writers as Lewis Carroll, Edward Lear, A.A. Milne, Kenneth Grahame, P.G. Wodehouse, Walter de la Mare, and Beatrix Potter withstood extra-literary considerations of the late nineteenth and twentieth centuries. Indeed, benign humor could only flourish in England.

The problem in developing a workable critical approach to the literature of the benign humorists is compounded by their use of language and confusion over what language should or should not do. Any *new* criticism, as a result, must recognize *new* ways to analyze the language and literature of the humorists of nineteenth- and twentieth-century England. Such new approaches, for example, must determine why the specific arrangement of thirteen letters in such a way that the word "sophisticated" is materialized is considered a more acceptable "literary usage" than the shorter but no less complex birth of five letters into one of P.G. Wodehouse's favorite words, "toney."

The benign humorists cared little for the yolk of traditional language. As a result they developed a language, consisting heavily of iconic signs, which defies linguistic answers borne of metaphorical linkages. The "make-up" languages of the humorists discourage and, in some cases, negate and render useless critical techniques and methodologies based on metaphor and literary historicism. It would be wrong, however, to view the language of the benign humorists as little more than a picnic spread, an afternoon-toot, an ingenuous roll-in-the-hay.

While the language of the humorists seems to be just busy being, it is clear to those willing to look closely into the comic vapors of their respective *oeuvres* that the language and resulting literature of the benign humorists says a great deal about nineteenth- and twentieth-century English society by saying nothing at all. In fact, benign humor emerges as both a literary and an "extraterritorial," extra-literary force. It is a force that demands critical reckoning.

For the modern reader especially such works as Lewis Carroll's *Alice in Wonderland,* Edward Lear's verses and limericks, Kenneth Grahame's *The Wind in the Willows,* P.G. Wodehouse's Bertie Wooster-Jeeves cycle of stories, Walter de la Mare's fantastic verses and songs, or Beatrix Potter's animal adventures suggest a sweet place in which to spend two hours. The humorists' work was a cheer hollered into the nineteenth and twentieth centuries. For the contemporary reader willing to listen, the cheer still reverberates.

The aspirations of the benign humorists were modest but their achievements are not. And where many modern writers of the literature of the genteel, the proletarian, the absurd, the Dada, the questing, the gothic, the dark and witty, etc., seem to have lost their way in the amazed, labyrinthian and abstract shuffle of the twentieth-century's roiling confusions, the benign-humorists produced a rescuing literature which promises to provide a respite from the twentieth-century's social incongruities and cultural-isms. Inevitably, the literature of the benign humorists as well as the writing of those writers more designedly escapist, such as Dorothy Sayers and Arthur Conan Doyle, offers the twentieth-century reader a way to get well, a way to stay well. As literature, the work of the nineteenth- and twentieth-century humorists is accomplished in both a literary and, not so curiously perhaps, therapeutic means. Indeed, the benign humorists produced a literature which promises to become the great artistic escape of the late twentieth century.

Acknowledgement

I would like to render full acknowledgement to those whose en-couragement and assistance brought *The Benign Humorists* to successful fruition. I acknowledge Stanly M. Vogel whose counsel and constructive advice were much appreciated. I would also like to thank Joseph T. Gavaghan and Nancy L. Bliss for their technical assistance in the preparation of the manuscript. Finally, I would like to acknowledge my debt to Steven B. Katz for his constant assistance in the preparation of all areas of the manuscript.

1.
The Literary Tradition of Wit and Humor

In *Ring For Jeeves,* P. G. Wodehouse's characters Bill Rowcester and his valet Jeeves once again find themselves in the bisque of things. It happens that Captain Biggar, one of Wodehouse's delightful "great White-Hunters" who pop up periodically in the humorist's stories, has been flim-flammed by Lord Rowcester disguised as a bookie. Rowcester, attempting to escape with Biggar's money, motors away with the hunter's last few dollars, earned on safari. Biggar, however, reads the license plate and traces the car back to the residence of Rowcester. Jeeves, trying to protect his master who has taken to placing bets in order to heat his baronial but water-soaked home, suggests that Biggar's eyesight had been in error when reading the license plate. Biggar responds with a show of bravado:

> I am Biggar the White Hunter, the most famous white hunter in all Africa and Indonesia. I can stand without a tremor in the path of an onrushing rhino and why? Because my eyesight is so superb that I know that I can get him in that one vulnerable spot before he has come within sixty paces. That's the sort of eyesight mine is.

Jeeves, annoyed by Biggar's conceit, responds:

> I fear I cannot recede from my position, sir. I grant that you may have trained your eyesight for such a contingency as you have described but, poorly informed as I am on the subject

1

of the larger fauna of the East, I do not believe that rhinoceri
are equipped with license numbers.[1]

To truly appreciate the humor implicit in Jeeves's droll retort, the reader should know something of the English tradition
perpetuated by those whom Wodehouse has called "great white
hunters." The reader should also recognize the countering force in
Jeeves's carefully worded rebuttal. Especially significant to an
understanding of the exchange is a knowledge of the social balance
maintained by English service. Jeeves, for example, knows that his
fish-fed brain is far in advance of his employer's, but he also realizes that his sardonic retort should be carefully couched in proper
English which is both gentle and cutting.

What Anthony Burgess calls "Ameriglish" and "Britglish"
jokes and comic stories vary significantly. Much American humor,
for example, has an intention and a dimension that makes it seem
hard. More often than not the humor turns anxious as it expresses
itself in anecdote and exaggeration. Although S. J. Perelman is not
an especially "American" writer, his book, *Acres and Pains,*
offers a delightful example of American humor. In *Acres and
Pains* Perelman tells of his difficulty with country living and with
the building of a swimming pool in particular.

> On the appointed morning, the place was busier than New
> London during the Harvard-Yale regatta. Whole clans of
> Mennonites and Amish bearing box lunches arrived from the
> back country in ancient buckboards. Sightseers wandered
> through the garden poking sly fun at our vegetables, and one
> bystander mimicked my gait and speech so cleverly that I
> could not help sharing the general merriment. When every-
> thing was ready, I retired to the tool shed with my family and
> made them lie flat on the floor. With a warning, "Stand clear
> all!" the dynamiter threw his switch. The blast which fol-
> lowed tore the roof off the springhouse and broke windows in
> the county seat sixteen miles away. Its only effect on the
> dam, however, was to harden the cement in it. My specialist
> bit his lip in chagrin. "I must have cut her a bit too fine," he
> confessed; "I'll fix her tomorrow, by cracky."
>
> He kept his word. When the dust finally settled, I had
> enough firewood for the next fifty years, most of it right inside
> the house where I could get at it. And when I finally settled,
> the man next door had a new front porch and a glass eye you

couldn't tell from the other one. Of course, it's a bit unwieldy for five people to take a bath in a washtub, particularly at one time, but at least you don't have to look out for copperheads.[2]

Perelman's story is delightful and humorous, but in a certain American way. The story's significant difference from the English humor exhibited in the exchange between Captain Biggar and Jeeves, is found in its building of momentum and in its incidence of exaggeration. For example, "... the place was busier than New London ...," "Whole clans of Mennonites ... arrived ...." Especially quick and exaggerated is Perelman's description of ushering his family into the tool shed where he tells them to lie down flat on the floor, etc. In the end, after the racket subsides, Perelman preciously remarks that at least "[we] don't have to look out for copperheads." And although Perelman has been one of America's more subtle humorists, *Acres and Pains* offers an American humor more sledgehammer than shy.

Unable to find full satisfaction in farce, folly, or even parody, many nineteenth- and twentieth-century American writers felt a need to garden wit, humor, and satire deep in the American experience, making it responsive to societal flow and cultural way. For the English writer of humor, however, the joke was the *way* of the joke. For the American writer, the joke was but the way to *get to* something or somebody extrinsic to the joke proper. For many nineteenth- and twentieth-century American writers, there was to be a very clear "revenge-factor" in any comic expression. But against their own societal and cultural contexts, both stories mentioned before could be considered humorous and "absurd."

Wit: *The Edge of Literary Humor*

Expressions of literary wit, unlike literary humor, are charged with message and fraught with circumstance. It is difficult, therefore, to settle on a singular, inclusive definition of literary wit. G. K. Chesterton, for instance, thought that wit "[was] reason on its judgement seat." Locke made a better toilet of it as he felt "wit lay in a quick association of ideas directed to show comparisons thereby producing pleasant pictures and agreeable visions in fancy." Hazlitt certainly did not lack "fancy" when he wrote, "wit is an illustration of heightened absurdities of life finding unexpected likeness in one thing to another." For Dryden, wit is "a propriety of thoughts and words."[3]

Walter Sorell, in his energetic yet patronizing book, *Facets of Comedy,* writes that "wit is basic to all comedy." Sorell, not unlike other academic purists, must have pedigree. His research of the etymological roots of "wit," adds very little information by which "wit" can be distinguished from other veins of literary humor. (Sorell is nothing if not doughty, and he points out that "witan" means to understand, the sanscrit "veda" means to have knowledge, while the German "wita" suggests Germanic intellectual acumen.)[4] To define wit and humor in an etymological manner, although a fit and charming repast, is unrewarding. In fact, it is impossible to *capture* a definition of wit through the resources of scholarly exposition and academic heurism. Such efforts serve only to salt the discovery trail. The trail, of course, leads only to the next bend.

Indeed, to define and analyze "wit" and "humor" is to be humorous. For example, in George Vasey's *The Philosophy of Laughing,* the chapters of the book begin with delightful illustrations of orotund, rotund, and even moribund folk and pub-crawlers who, according to Vasey show, *by their appearance,* "degrees of humor [wit]." These "degrees," according to Vasey, can be detected and categorized in those who "scientifically exhibit:"

1. The Benevolent Smile
2. The Giggling Laugh
3. The Obstreperous Laugh
4. The Hearty Laugh of the Gentle Sex
5. The Stentorian Laugh of the Stronger Sex
6. The Superlative Laugh (or that laugh which exhibits a high degree of something or other.)

Vasey does not let the subject alone until he makes his bid for literary immortality in a chapter entitled, "On the Baleful Effects of Tickling and Otherwise Improperly Handling Children in Which the Reproductive Organs are Excited and Prematurely Developed."[5]

In many cases, the literary presentation of wit is an expression by writers who have failed in their attempt to write a "purer," more sublime form of humor. American writers of "light literature," especially, tired from overusing Mark Twain's comic repertoire, obligingly accepted the intoxicating yet easy accomplishments of "wit." But nineteenth- and twentieth-century writers of wit were unable to do what Addison and Steele did—temper wit with good nature. For the nineteenth- and twentieth-century English writer of light prose, badinage and quick retort were never enough. Consequently, they developed a humor which took "18th century social consciousness and sense of ridicule and [turned] it to 'amiability' . . . ."[6]

Max Eastman suggests that American humor had always been more congenial than English humor and, as far as he was concerned, English humorists and wits "did little" for social harmony as they tended to be what the critic calls "cruelly sarcastic and cold." Eastman's conclusions are inappropriate when applied to England's more benign humorists. If confined to England's literary wits, Eastman's comment is correct enough. Evan Esar, in an attempt to isolate wit and humor within England's comic tradition, alludes to the most consummate comic literature as those expressions of the "wisecrack," "the epigram," "the riddle," "the conundrum," "the gag," "the joke," and "the anecdote."[7]

Stephen Leacock, more cognizant of the inherent pitfalls in any attempt to categorize humor, could not resist dealing with a literature which he saw as "the humor . . . of situation," "the humor of character," "the humor of comic verse," and "the nonsense verse or prose."[9] Leacock, however, has upgraded and updated critical approaches to humor and wit, making it more possible to draw proper distinctions between the two. Leacock's original work in the area of humor includes a theory which he labels "the sense of sound." Leacock refers to the greatest humorists as those writers who use words which "have tones of subconscious sound appeal."[9]

Certainly this "sense of sound" is best rendered by the accomplished humorists who seemed to pick the "wrong word" for the
sense but the "right word" for the *sound*. (In this regard, one suspects, P. G. Wodehouse's mystical valet Jeeves could not have
been called anything else since the *sound* of the name when delivered down the valet's nose makes so much *sense* in light of the
characterization.) The writer of wit, on the other hand, searches
assiduously for just the "right word," the mot juste, the bon mot.
For the writer of wit it is paramount, if not "tanta," for the chosen
word to be keen and cuttingly accurate.

English Humor and American Wit

To always search and court the "right word" is not to say that
the writer of wit is more "serious" about his craft than is the
humorist. It is also inappropriate to conclude that the *search* for
the "right word" is so intrinsic to the creative process that the
search and *seizure* alone measures accuracy of statement and
degree of artistry. The wit's search for incisive comment which
must balance on the cut and blade of their uncertain art, must be
undertaken by metaphorical linkage that allows the literary humorist to communicate the *point* of his language. The humorists, however, are unconcerned with what seems to them the "surdity" of
such a search. (The humorists, however, never dismiss the seminal
appeal of absurdity, and one suspects that they would enjoy and
appreciate the efforts of such meridian humorists as McLuhan and
Edmund Carpenter. Carpenter, in an essay, "Acoustic Space,"
points out that "thereafter," and such words as "before," "space,"
and "interval of time," have a *spatial meaning* which should not
suggest "sight."[10] Such theoretical fragrance as this, of course, is
plash in the mainstream of a benign humor which makes few points
about things that don't need points made at all.)

The humorist's art is more instinctual than heuristic. His work, however, does not suffer from a lack of cognition. The humorists would have no difficulty intuiting that the expression "the night is filled with music" is a funny visual as well as a linguistic conundrum and material implausibility. The humorist, however, would *know* that conclusions about "night music" are funny because so unnecessary and academic. The writer of wit, however, would be tempted to take the error implicit in the expression "the night is filled with music," and "do something about it."

The humorists have always left surface dread and "problems" to the satirists and wits. The sublime humorists have felt, as Wodehouse continues to feel, that cultural problems and social dilemmas are so much seed-in-the-wind. The humorists, as a result, never had to look into the malaise and flux of the nineteenth and twentieth centuries. To the humorist, "malaise" is but a "proper rhyme" for "mayonnaise." It is left to the literary wit to test the air for determining winds. Frequently, they are gulled into blowing back at the wind.

Humor is a reward at the beginning and at the end of the comic rainbow while wit is the literary aspirant located somewhere along the spectrum, a lesser literature, if only in terms of its lack of completion and finish. Perhaps the most satisfying examples of wit are those which seem straightforward but which, on closer examination, reveal the sharpness of a nearly hidden message. For example, G. K. Chesterton, when writing affectionately about nonsense humor states ". . . pure nonsense . . . is a holiday of the mind."[12] George Orwell displays an escalating wit when he compares Lewis Carroll to Edward Lear. Orwell writes, "The writer closest to Lear [in the expression of nonsense] . . . was Lewis Carroll who, however, was less essentially fantastic . . ."[13] Orwell's declaration seems straightforward enough; although to compare Carroll *to* Lear rather than Lear to Carroll is a conscious expression of that wit which seems to hide in innocuous statement. Wit is an expression in transit. When it stops, as it must, to load up on commentary and venom—poisons cultured in and disguised by literary erudition—it chills, becomes warped, clipped, and rather nasty. Wit, unlike the more sublime humor, is rarely deep going even though its fuss and fury are admirable if simply as an exercise in verbal pyrotechnics. Wit, even more than satire, is noisy—a racket "too often personal, malicious, diabolic, or political . . . a stick to beat a dog."[11]

But humor can be a confused reward. Evan Esar has made a scrupulous if self-defeating attempt to analyze the linguistic properties of humor. In fact, his book, *The Humor of Humor,* signals a call for a "more scholarly approach" to the study and critique of humor. Esar suggested calling this specialized study "humorology" and recommended the development of a "humorous etymology." Although well-intentioned, Esar's and other like approaches to the humorists must be chastised and turned back lest they claim analytical success. The literature of humor depends, after all, on the near-impossibility and clear implausibility of ever finding any one reliable methodology.

Distinctions between the literature of American humor and English humor indicate that there is about both humors a generic, almost organic quality which gives each a distinct and hereditary quality. For late nineteenth- and twentieth-century American writers of comic literature, there never seems to have been a plethora of people or institutions that seemed all that funny.

By the end of the nineteenth century, things began to look bleak and quite desperate to the writers of comic literature in America. The comic literati in America was further inhibited by having to draw upon their own meagre senses of humor—a small reserve which had something less than two centuries in which to gather. History yielded little in the way of comic personages and the American writer was perceptive enough to see that Cottons and Increase's of Mather were not exactly the prototypes upon which to build a literary humor—especially a humor without the malice and considerable sting of wit. The quickness of the nineteenth century melted into the techno-implosions of the twentieth century, giving neither time nor heart to the American humorist. Therefore, to combat dun-colored memories of young but stern pasts and color-less people, and to impede the steely quickening of science, the American humorist became a wit—a sort of masterjack, trading in problems and using them to score American culture. Wit, in fact, was easier to come by. But it is a testimony to literary resourcefulness that this wit could have its borders trimmed in humor, provided that the writer had a good ear for dialect and regional speech eccentricities. These rather infrequent instances of humor came straight out of the oral tradition implicit in "Twain's folk-narratives, Benchley's and Thurber's city-folk talks," Dorothy Parker's "big-blonde folk and big brunette folk with big-city problems talk."[14] Indeed, by the 1960s the oral tradition of humor in America would be, in part, maintained by a proliferation of oral meta-speaks and alternative languages, all manifest in such literary mutations as "soul-dictionaries," "goyim glossaries," and the like. Even though they add little humor to the present age, one suspects that Van Wyck Brooks, at least, would have been pleased with such flashy but unstudied nativism.

Where the English "saw eccentricity as their birth-right," Americans found erratic behavior distasteful, and certainly not the stuff of humor.[15] Adult foibles and adolescent remissions were not especially "funny." As a result, the comic literature of the nineteenth and twentieth centuries in America was posited with the wits since they seemed better equipped to deal with an "unfunny society." But their literature qua wit qua journalism was selfishly cultivated and rather exclusively rendered. The literature of the wits was published almost exclusively in publications called "smart magazines." Such magazines included, among others, *Smart Set, The New Yorker, Vogue,* and *Vanity Fair.* The "smart magazines," however, did not appeal to the populace at large and had little allure for readers outside urban areas. Indeed, readers in Kansas had scant need for citified chic and sophisticated soirees. As a result, the literary wit who published in the "smart magazines" seemed to be telling most Americans perhaps unwittingly, that they were stupid. By the 1930s, however, H. L. Mencken's "booboise" were in no mood to laugh and could ill-afford even the most half-hearted smile. In fact, as the twentieth century flashed forward, Americans were hard-pressed to indulge anything even remotely like a "sense-of-humor." Even the efforts of such "funny people" as Dorothy Parker seemed flat and vapid—nothing more than journalistic vamping. Parker's one-liners, such as "Verlaine was always chasing Rimbauds," meant little to the reader corny in Topeka, and the reader scrambling for food in New York.

Carolyn Wells suggests that humor invested in literature is a matter of "national character." She writes that [Americans] are quick, deft, nervous, energetic; therefore, their sense of fun finds expression in the nimble exercise of wit. The English take everything much more seriously; therefore their sense of fun finds expression in the more serious and dignified exercise of humor."[16] But even as likeable a scholar as Wells has reservations about literary humor. Wells, however, hedges her bets somewhat when she writes that "a sense of humor is an appreciation of a happy misfit in the eternal fitness of things. . . . [while] wit is the verbal expression of a sense of humor."[17] Wells, like most "sophisticated" American readers is, at the very least, ambivalent about the contributions, significance, and artistry of the literature of humor.

The American expression of humor in the writings of nineteenth- and twentiety-century wits served as a means by which they could debunk a society in which people lived in the fear of being debunked. As a result, the literature of the wits tended to grate on rather than humor people. Too frequently, the wits saw the apogee of literary endeavor in witty, clever, and mean remarks. But still the niggling question remains—why were comic literati in America more at home with the expression of wit? E. J. Oliver sheds an incredible light on the question when he writes, "Christian conception is based on goodness, the rationalist on intelligence, so that the Christian values innocence as the rationalist prizes knowledge."[18] Oliver, writing about wit and humor, seems to imply that since England is more populated with Christians (in terms of percentage), and since the Christians have been there longer than they have been in America, it is inevitable that humor—the "innocent factor" in the comic tradition—would be more effectively realized in England. Indeed, "faith" is not the least effective way to accept the literature of the American wits. The wits quite clearly depend on and encourage the faith of their readers and listeners. But still the wit-as-raconteur feels the need to predispose the audience for the expression of wit. For example, before a joke or comic story is launched, the audience is "reassured" with such rhetorical balms as "Trust me, you'll like this one," or "You'll really get a kick out of this," or, more indelicately, "You'll die laughing when you hear this one." Of course a literary wit's intention is never so literal; to draw blood is enough.

Sheer Uplift: Nineteenth- and Twentieth-Century English Humor

The English humorists had wit enough to know that a humor more benign than wit would be more charming and perhaps, graceful in a time searching for aesthetic and societal charity. Unlike American humor, which grew and festered in wit alone, English humor, by the mid-nineteenth century, found new expression. This new and more benign humor gave a lift to the English people suffering through the same sag of nerve and the same lack of intellectual and cultural direction as the Americans. The English, however, would have less truck with pessimism.

J. B. Priestley addresses the rather curious English monopoly on what shall be called "benign humor." For Priestley and others,

> The English humor (unlike the public air of French wit) is curiously private and domestic, offering nothing to the casual arrival from other countries; it is a part of the atmosphere of the place, a hazy light on things; it manifests itself in innumerable slow grins and chuckles; it is not something that can be picked up with the language, but something that must be given time to filter through; and thus while it is everywhere, a traveller in a hurry might well be excused for not noticing that it is here at all.[19]

Indeed, there is an insularity about the nineteenth- and twentieth-century literature of English humor which keeps it safe from unrewarding and unaccomplished criticisms. The English humorist cultivated an inner-weather—humor bred selectively "in the souls," or thereabouts, of people being sniffed at by intellectuals and harangued by the labor unions. Life was steeling as it tested the mettle of the English to see if they could survive a "nasty time" which, of course, did not obviate the need for a sense of humor.

The late nineteenth- and early twentieth-century English humorist did not assume the role of humorist without a considerable history. Indeed, the pre-nineteenth-century battle was fought on uncertain fields with the darker legions of wit and satire flanked and belligerent. By the nineteenth century, however, the air would clear. A definition for this new humor was crystallizing, and J. B. Priestley writes, "[English humor] is where melancholy and mirth play like light and shadow . . . a mind once robbed of its bloom and golden haze is utterly without charm [and gives] us the leaden-eyed Englishman of the satirists." But even the English satire seemed little more than a "tender mockery."

Nineteenth- and twentieth-century English literary humor is often governed by risible phrases and delightfully hazy minds, both charmingly unintellectual in nature. This, of course, makes the humor even more incomprehensible to an elite corps of fin de siècle critics who have realized that this new literary humor was best measured in jackknife handles than by numbers of analytical cuts. Priestley is correct when he remarks that the English "think in fun while they feel in earnest." Of course, the importance of being earnest was that it precluded insincere, critical incursions into the literature of the humorists while, at the same time, it encouraged the humorists to keep safe the "inner weather" of their most remarkable genre. The English humorists nourished themselves.

The English sense of humor could be sardonic while promising little blade. Indeed, the English seemed fonder of a humor *sans* wit—a humor without bile. But still by the twentieth century, the humorists would be outranked and seemingly outwritten by satirists such as the very social Evelyn Waugh and Aldous Huxley as well as those journalists and humorists writing for such magazines as *Punch* and *Strand*. To the English critics, however, almost any sort of writer in the comic vein outran the more sublime humorists. But the humorists took heart in the knowledge that out-of-sorts antiquarians rarely like anything anyway. In the late nineteenth and early twentieth centuries, however, there was another sort of humor being written which, at first glance, seems mean at heart and intentionally cruel. But even this humorous bitchery, unlike the sharper thrusts of such Algonquin wits as

Dorothy Parker, Alexander Woolcott, Robert Benchley, et al., seems more kittenish than feline. The main practitioners of the English humor of bitchery are Oscar Wilde, Noel Coward, James McNeill Whistler, W. S. Gilbert, Beerbohm Tree, Max Beerbohm and G. K. Chesterton. (But while sharp wit seems the literary staple of such writers, there are few better examples of the gentle, sublime humor of the more benign humorists than Noel Coward's arch but merely fussy play *Hay Fever.*)

The Americans, of course, developed the same qualities of bitch-in-humor, but there was little doubt, excepting the efforts of S. N. Behrman, that theirs was an attempted literature best left to the English to write. The English humorists, after all, knew of what they were speaking as they actually lived—carte-blanche—in country homes and Regency apartments. It mattered little that they hardly ever owned them, and it mattered not at all that they were constantly on the sponge. The writers of "bitcherese" in America had less sense of place as they drank their lunches in various bars, leaning on each other, funny as crutches, wondering why they hadn't been born English. Even their stories had something faintly British about them. Robert Benchley, a dues paying Algonquinite, "luvved" Dorothy Paker's one-liner about "the American starlet who broke her leg sliding down a barrister." For Benchley, it was "veddy."

The English humorist in the "bitch-tradition," however, knew how to smother the devastations of wit in masquerades which were never allowed to overstay their visit. Even the nastiest of the English humorists winced at and called "rum" the tactlessness displayed in such Americanisms as H. L. Mencken's "no one ever went broke underestimating the American public." When dealing with subjects seemingly geared to bring out the worst in them (such as America and Americans), the "humorists-of-bitchery couch round their darting *oeuvre* with words and phrases that lead the discreet and careful reader to the realization that, at bottom, these humorists harbored, at least a closet affection for many Americanisms. For example, when referring to jargon in *Cakes and Ale,* Maugham writes, "The Americans who are the most efficient people on earth, have carried this device [use of jargon] to such a height of perfection and have invented so wide a range of pithy and hackneyed phrases, that they can carry on an amusing conversation without giving a moment's reflection to what they are saying and so leave their minds free to consider the more important matters of big business and fornication."[21]

The difference between the American and English apprehension and use of the comic tradition in nineteenth- and twentieth-century literature can be seen in reactions to a passage written by a writer who can rightfully be called both an English and American humorist. Using the literature of P. G. Wodehouse—certainly one of the most sublime of all humorists—a class of American students in a "Modern English Literature" course were asked to analyze a dialogue between Wodehouse's perpetually moon-struck Bertie Wooster and "his man" Jeeves. The young master awakes.

> Good evening, Jeeves
> "Good morning, sir."
> This surprised me.
> Is it morning?
> "Yes, sir,"
> Are you sure, it seems very dark outside?
> "There is a fog, sir, if you will recollect, we are now in Autumn season of mists and mellow fruitfullness."
> Oh, yes, I see. Well be that as it may, get me one of those bracers of yours, will you?[22]

After being *told* that the passage was "delightful" and "very humorous," the students were asked both to indicate *where* the humor in the passage was and asked to interpret *why* it seemed humorous. Out of the class of thirty-five, not one student was able to discern and analyze the alleged humor in the intercourse between Wooster and Jeeves. Indeed, for the entire class, the passage seemed profoundly unhumorous. Indeed, what the instructor saw as "befuddlement," the class tended to see as "stupidity." In addition, the class saw the clipped and rather delightfully polished remarks of the valet to be but an expression of someone "rather effete." In almost all cases the class's analysis of the passage was done quite literally, as one student put it, with "[an] eye out" for the "reality of the passage." The American interpretation seems clear enough—if the humor is not embedded experientially, if it is without a metaphorical base, thus implausible in terms of connection to past readings, the Wodehousian passage is not humorous and, in fact, rather un-American.

It is equally clear that American literary humor—in order to gain validity as literature and significance as message—has somehow to be *pointed*. It has to *mean*. Indeed, it is difficult for many American readers to see the *point* of much English humor—the *point*, of course, being that the humor *not* be pointed at all. In fact, the more benign humorists of late nineteenth- and early twentieth-century England wrote a literature that remains *pointedly* pointless.

There are ways, however, to deal with the pointedly pointless. For example, an English instructor who found Kenneth Grahame's *The Wind in the Willows* rather meaningless when read alone, delighted in reading it *aloud* to his wife, after which she would, on a successive week, read it back to him *aloud*. Such oral procedure, of course, is not just an attempt to recapture the utility of the oral tradition more implicit in American Literature, it is also an attempt to *materialize* and *make entities* out of the humorous language by putting sound into it and then filling the air with it. Although such procedure can enhance the reading of Grahame's story, it does not, in and of itself, insure a grasp of the special language. In fact, even such a humorist as Marshall McLuhan could have told the English instructor that "air cannot be *filled* that way."

2.
Nineteenth- and Twentieth-Century English Wits and Humorists

The development of the literary humorists must be viewed against the social, cultural and intellectual climate of nineteenth and twentieth-century England. Such a consideration, along with a core understanding of the comic tradition in England since the Restoration, reveals the reasons and need for a literature written by those who shall be called "benign humorists." Such humorists developed a literature which asks for critical consideration free and isolated from the very same conditions that, indirectly at least, helped forge their art. Most literary artists, however, have never been completely successful in escaping society's fish-bowl vision and cultural coils. A writer must, after all, use the language formulated and developed by the society in which he or she lives and from which they are destined to gather their material. Societal and cultural conditions, by the fin de siècle, suggested different art forms, new literatures. And just beneath the traumatic and thin gel of the late nineteenth and early twentieth century, many of the literati retooled their art in order to shape new aesthetics, new dialectics, and new theories which would, no matter how obliquely, address modernity. Not many would succeed.

Late nineteenth-century England faced a challenge to its class structure—a challenge based on the steady erosion of upper class wealth and dictated in part by the burgeoning numbers consigned to the lower middle and lower classes. These "lowering" classes settled in and around cities as an industrial revolution began to transform the environment into ungracious gouges and dispirited digs.

By the late nineteenth century, with the cultural flow beginning to push slowly against Victorianism, the intellectuals seemed to lose their cultural locus in the gathering ash of an already burnt-out time. In the twentieth-century dawn, England tried to shake out the "irreligious revelations" of Darwinism. But this "new puzzlement" took root, and it was accompanied by the expanding drifts and woods of fringe-thinks and alternative-cultures. In the universities, a "balkanization of thought" set in as education "began to specialize mental life."[23] The mannered Victorian intellectuals—used to "good talk" and other accoutrements of jade—began to lose their artistic raison d'etre as society turned unabashedly toward new sciences and arts to answer old dilemmas. It became devastatingly probable that the literature of the period might have to recognize new forms that might even come from slums and factories rather than residing in the more rarefied but comfortable homes of imagination and fancy. The more resourceful literary intellectuals and writers knew that finger-bussing and sashaying manners were not as theoretically viable as before. But when they saw imagination attacked by incestuous specialties and the nineteenth- and twentieth-century codification of life and thought, many regrouped, re-trenched, and withdrew their imaginative and considerable art from the new and harsh realities. The anglicized Pole, Joseph Conrad, presented the darkening times with *The Heart of Darkness,* while William Butler Yeats stated the idea of the Great Year. James Joyce refused linguistic codifications while T. S. Eliot saw the spread of *The Wasteland.* Other intellectuals, however, would agree to nourish the realities of "new" logics, alternative aesthetics.

While the "impetus of machinery" seemed to be "to produce supplementary machinery," many intellectuals began to react to the new hardware which was mucking up the Victorian sense of tidiness.[24] They saw micro-speech and sub-thoughts put unattractive rents in the silk, lace, and damask of a withering memory, a losing time. As a result, many writers equated literary experimentation with contemporaneity. Such experimentation, however, was limited by the realities of urban living as the city became the nexus between writer and materials. Time, birth, death, reincarnation, and love squatted thematically in the cities. Many writers resisted the new themes, however, as they were sure they remained the custodians of culture. Indeed, there seemed to be something pathetic and rather too precious about those writers who placed their art on rusticating lawns—lawns then too high for mowing as service, along with those, whom some saw as lower-class comrades, moved to cities. To many writers and intellectuals, the times seemed to conspire against order and the imagination they preferred to cultivate in narrower Victorian gardens. Many intellectuals were, by the late nineteenth century, confused and ill-prepared for a constant flow of events. As a result, many intellectuals admitted the futility of old visions they saw crack in the reflections of an ugly time, a hopeless puzzle the utilitarians called progress, equality, and, alas, a new era. The more pessimistic writers and aestheticians foresaw the dawn of what they thought was a culture and literature based on the illogic of equal chance and easy accomplishments.

By the turn of the century, American intellectuals had their own problems. The English intellectuals, however, in the process of being stripped of "a more genteel way of life," saw, in America, a country where their fellow intellectuals appointed themselves "custodians of culture" in order to preserve for themselves what the English intellectuals seemed to have already lost. But where the "new philosophies" and alternative religions and art forms so confused the English, American ideas of modernity were somewhat "slanty" as well. For example, there seemed to be something distinctly American about a phenomenon which dictated a worship of youth. The English intellectuals were disheartened by the Americans who seemed to insist on finding answers bunched among the sinews and brash muscles of the very young. Even the intellectuals of America were young. They were not, however, any less disappointed in the flux and confusion of the late nineteenth and twentieth centuries than were their English counterparts. Many English intellectuals were further confused by what

art to wit and satire. Goldsmith[...]
ists, would also write journa[...]
"gemmed and small novels." M[...]
can write and wants out of ed[...]
ically but carefully, wrote wit[...]
no mark as he became the eig[...]
success. Indeed, Sheridan wro[...]
and demanded — perfect pla[...]
language. Even Byron, und[...]
Sheridan had written noth[...]
School For Scandal), the[...]
best farce (*The Critic*). F[...]
dan, some of it delivered l[...]
small amount of jealousy[...]
humor of the period. For[...]
table songs are always a[...]
ing wine, he was thoroug[...]

By the early nineteent[...]
would begin its drift tov[...]
1800s a more benign h[...]
better examples of this[...]
Smith's delightful story[...]
Referring to the 1824 [...]
itable Dame," Smith [...]

Dame Partingtor[...]
. . . squeezing ou[...]
the Atlantic Oc[...]
She was excelle[...]
have meddled v[...]

But by the mid-n[...]
the most necessa[...]
creased frequencie[...]
and serene. The [...]
bridge the eighte[...]
be clever, smart,[...]
achievement. Th[...]
who received cr[...]

---

many of them saw as the interesting but stupefying logic by which
many Americans, as one put it, translated money into material
superiority and then translated that into moral righteousness.
The English writer and intellectual gave up the ghost-like
search, realizing that answers to artistic and intellectual dilemmas were not necessarily to be found outside England. If they
had to, they would invent their own answers to their own dilemmas.

Literary Roots of England's Comic Tradition

From 1850 to 1875 there were years of relative prosperity and
Queen Victoria ruled well, if tightly, over a dominion of family
units. But Victorian society was ambiguously wrought. So, while
individualism was encouraged and frequently asserted, Victorian
society never really learned to trust the "individual intellectual."
The society—in Victorian England an unclear entity at best—
proved it could ignore those who "marched to the syncopations
of thought and mind." Therefore, many of the intellectuals
fell to bickering among themselves. Macaulay, for example, de-
nounced Matthew Arnold as the "great apostle of the Philistines"
while, in the next breath, he glorified "the idea of utility."
Prone to pontificating, Macaulay required that literature be more
than a "deceptive fancy."[25] In the nineteenth century there
was no absence of disagreement, and while Trollope built a reportage out of correct postures, the presence of silk, and the
incidence of manners, Thomas Hardy rang restricted chimes for
the "toiling classes."

By the nineteenth century, the English were developing what
Priestley and others call a "modern sense of humor," and while
the years 1868-1880 brought the constancy of amusement with
Gladstone and Disraeli, they would be followed by Queen Vic-

toria's death which, o|
nalled an end to some|
century became more
over the Empire and |
But the English intell|
A good thing, for b|
ability to walk like |
swinging his cane |
machinations of t|
hard, the English|
small measure ha|
of their comic lite|

The comic trad|
Restoration to t|
the comic tradi|
clever, causticit|
some satires. F|
bine wit and|
Matthew Prio|
dan, Smollett|
creetly and|
William Th|
wits," Thacl|
miserable, r|
the Restor|
spirit in th|
and shrie|
Congreve|
plays tha|
people d|
John|
was like|
that wa|
the lite|
nial th|
praise|
Du|
write|

scholars who still equated clever phrases and stinging remarks with the practice of "serious literature." The most available forum for mid-nineteenth-century wit was the unpredictably "smart" magazine, *Punch*. And, although the magazine espoused the nineteenth-century's radical chic and cutting statement along with devastating political and social satires, there were the beginnings of an "easier" literature which did not shove and force for laughs. The magazine's editors were destined not to cast their lot with either the wits and satirists or the more benign humorists as *Punch* preferred to remain "fragmentary, hopping cheerfully from abuse to abuse."31

Albert Smith's column in *Punch* entitled "Physiologies" surveyed the indolent idlers who huddled pub-like out in the mist of London and around lamp posts; fellow-writer Shirley Brooks countered with sketches about the urbane and witty in England's higher society. No less significant a contribution to the comic tradition of the nineteenth century were the illustrations of John Leech and Charles Keane.

The magazine was not especially predisposed toward the more amiable and sublime humorists in the years from 1857 to 1874 when the magazine staff divided into Liberal and Conservative party camps. The 1860s, however, did see the emergence of Francis Burnaud, who wrote a deft prose called "spoof-journalism." Through Burnaud's efforts in the years from 1874 to 1880, *Punch* turned a gay blade as "fine and sublime" spirits were supplied to those whom Burnaud felt were *Punch's* new readership—"scholars and gentlemen." In 1880, Burnaud took over editorship of the magazine, and almost immediately it became kinder and more congenial. But it was not always easy to delineate wit from the less malignant humor in *Punch*. *Punch's* humor has been described as ". . . [coming] from three main sources. First comes a jealously guarded quirk in a semi-hermit, a private joke matured in isolation and often developed over the years as an escape from life. Then there is the journalist's humor, the sharp eye for what is going on. . . . Lastly, there is humor that springs from the meeting of private amusement and public fact in a social setting."32

Clearer about what constituted humor-in-wit were the "Cambridge Wits"—academics and writers, but more often talkers, who felt it had been left to them to protect and foster the element of wit in the English comic tradition.

The "Cambridge wits" restricted their comic expression to the more certain charms of Cambridge University as they found little to cheer them in the "hoipolloi" outside the ivy who had to "actually grub" for bread-stuffs and turnips. According to one of its members, the "Cambridge Wits" were the elite comedians "who . . . were up with us in the great days . . . [who] assisted in those splendid triumphs on the river [Cam]; wore fancy waistcoats or those aggressive trousers . . . [and had] midnight talks when the pipes were relighted and the coffee bubbled on the hob . . ."[33] Fortunately, the "Cambridge Wits" exhausted their strings of linguistic bon-bons and mots juste in excessive conversation before they could turn it into literature. To be sure, the wit of the Cambridgians was very much in its oral delivery.

Charles Stuart Calverley, a fellow-wit "who had gone wrong with poetry," exhibited a delightful and wistful humor he would activate at the most extraordinary times. Typical of his quintessential wit are the minutes Calverley kept of a Cambridge faculty meeting. In the minutes, Calverley lists the meeting's "highpoints" in the resolutions,

Master	That no people give so much trouble, if you try to extract money from them, as solicitors.
Junior Dean	Except, perhaps, Parsons.
Senior Dean	The latter possibly because they have not got the money.
Mr. A	That a ton of weight is a great deal of books.
Mr. B	That it is just one o-clock.
Mr. C	That, that it is likely that in an hour it will be just two.[34]

At such faculty assemblies were fellow-wits John Sterling, Alexander Kinglake, Edward Fitzgerald, and Richard Monckton Milnes, whom, everyone agreed, "had a great talent" for conversation.

Nineteenth- and Twentieth-Century Wits

As the nineteenth century moved toward its final wind, the wits were pinched by the times and their own reputations. James McNeill Whistler, for instance, becomes quite difficult as he objects to ". . . the place of his birth, the year of his birth, and his second baptismal name." (Lowell, Massachusetts, one suspects, has since forgiven Whistler his indiscreet objections.) But Whistler was another of the fringe-humorists who polished their uncertain artistry for the sparkles of conversation. It was typical Whistler who, when questioned whether he thought genius was hereditary, answers, "I can't tell you, Heaven has granted me no off-spring."[35] But while his close friends Dante Rossetti and Swinburne admired his portraits and etchings, they were also forced to read—in the name of friendship—Whistler's malicious prose which he published in 1890 under the title *The Gentle Art of Making Enemies.* Unfortunately, Whistler would produce another book called *The Baronet and the Butterfly.* Almost everyone wished he hadn't.

William S. Gilbert was both wicked and talented, and it seemed that everyone earned his disfavor at one time or another. Once, after noticing that his "friend" Beerbohm Tree was "actually sweating" during the performance of Tree's comedy *Engaged,* Gilbert, unimpressed by the play's cast, remarks "[well] your skin has been acting at all events."[36] Gilbert, unlike Whistler, wore well, and after the production of his fantasy plays, *The Palace of the Truth* and *The Wicked World,* had a long string of arch, dodging plays of which he was the composer and librettist for the playwright, Arthur Sullivan. Within the genre of comic opera Gilbert dominated and had no peers.

The nineteenth-century wits were versatile, and while they were frequently cold and repellent, they were also undeniably hilarious. Oscar Wilde, after four "entrancing years" at Oxford, became the most consummate practitioner of this curiously balanced wit. For example, after being told that "Christopher Columbus was a great man," Wilde, quite innocently but with his tongue-in-cheek, inquired why that was so? The man answered "because Columbus had discovered America." Wilde retorts

"Oh, no, it had often been discovered before, but it was always hushed up."[37]

By 1883, Wilde was firmly established as England's resident raconteur and most accomplished and convivial ne'er-do-well. At tea parties and behind lecterns, however, much of Wilde's wit was lost in enervating conversations. But, unlike the "Cambridge Wits," Wilde was a peripatetic litterateur as he edited magazines (*Woman's World*, 1887-1891), wrote toy plays (*The Happy Prince*, 1888, and *A House of Pomegranates*, 1891), all the while sustaining constant conversation which he kept warm on the sideburners of his artistry. Wilde could criss and cross literary lines and his wit panned and flashed then quieted down in such essays as "The Soul of Man Under Socialism." But the amalgam of wit and mature artistry was strongest in his plays — *Lady Windermere's Fan* (1892), *A Woman of No Importance* 1893), and *The Importance of Being Earnest* (1893). And if Wilde seemed broken by his prison experience—a cruel test of his artistry which resulted in *Ballad of Reading Gaol*—he knew what even his severest critics were forced to admit about him: "we were never so entertained in our lives."

Hillaire Belloc's works run a continuum from historical treatises and Catholic tracts to witty songs and rather banal and vapid tales. Still one more Oxonian, Belloc wrote novels which frequently and quite unintentionally turned into historical treatises. Belloc, less successful than Goldsmith and Wilde, similarly refused to be restricted to specific milieu. Unlike the work of Wilde and Goldsmith, however, Belloc's works were literary picnic spreads set and hampered by a writer who would never stop thinking of becoming a lawyer, or even a seaman. Unfortunately, some critical ants would niggle over and nibble his works until they carried off much of Belloc's reputation.

Tittering forth from Oxford (apparently, like Cambridge in the nineteenth century, a very funny place) came Max Beerbohm. In the 1890s Beerbohm did humorous caricatures for the magazine *Strand*. Not too many of course, for Beerbohm strongly suspected that it was still fashionable to be indolent and rather "underemployed." In 1896, however, Beerbohm published a book of essays which he imaginatively and modestly called *The Works of Max Beerbohm.* Beerbohm was, like his fellow wits and dilettantes, restless with, and unconvinced by, any one skill and specific genre. As a result, Beerbohm took over from George Bernard Shaw when the latter retired as drama critic for *The Saturday Review.* Fashionably unimpressed, Beerbohm writes ". . . that [I] got the job at all is amazing since [I] never regarded theatre as much more than the conclusion to dinner or the prelude to a supper."[38] In 1912, Beerbohm began to settle some accounts, and he subsequently wrote a curious and diverting book of parodies called *A Christmas Garland.*

Gilbert Keith Chesterton's wit was brittle, if more seminally bizarre than most. His more remarkable efforts, *The Man Who Was Thursday* (1908), *Manalive* (1911), and *The Flying Inn* (1914), seem to be fantasies winging, not on wit and other terminal fancies, but on ideas conceived and fashioned in the blue-heavens which rattled about his bulbous head. Chesterton's more sublime humor and wit, however, are realized in his easy and arcane "analogies." For example, when addressing "modern philosophers" and "journalists," who were inclined to give their preposterous assertions in parentheses, as if they were insignificant and unworthy of full expression, Chesterton parodies them by writing, "in two hundred years time, (when the individual consciousness is merged in the communal)." Indeed, Chesterton is an avenging editor who deplores his own parodies, such as "In 1649, King Charles I was condemned to be executed by a council presided over by Bradshaw (whose mother was a walrus)", or, "My home is in Beaconsfield, which is seven miles from High Wycombe and four miles from Gerrards Cross (where I ate ninety negroes. . . .)"[39]

Much of the nineteenth-century's light literature appeared in a "little magazine" called *The Spirit Lamp.* The *Lamp,* however, was extinguished shortly after Lord Alfred Douglas, Oscar Wilde's friend and patron of the arts, purchased it. Few tears were shed over its demise, however, and as one wag put it when informed that the magazine was about to be renewed early in the twentieth century, "We hope that this is not true, we did not like 'The Spirit Lamp.' "[40]

By the 1920s, literary wit would freeze, and out of the cold was written *Point Counter Point*. Aldous Huxley, unlike the wits of the nineteenth century, would not keep his ironies soft and a-loft as they collapse in "the tinsel and tears" of the twentieth century. Indeed, wit was to be redefined into something quite a bit uglier than what the nineteenth-century wits had in mind. Such a writer as Rose Macaulay would be called a "wit in the modern sense." Macaulay, unwittingly but accurately, reveals the temper of the writer of twentieth-century wit when she has one of her characters say, "she knows everything and felt nothing—like God."[51] Indeed, it was a wit caved-in to the times.

Indeed, the literary and Cambridge wits felt forced to *make* literature and talk directly out of the material offered by their age. The humorists, on the other hand, felt little need to battle the times or even respond to them. They felt no need to make social comment. Such freedom of thought and literary aesthetic escaped the wits as they remained tied to the age, influenced by extraliterary considerations.

Development of a Benign Humor

It is relatively easy to recognize and acknowledge the literary wits of the late nineteenth and early twentieth centuries; it is infinitely more difficult, however, to discern just who the more benign humorists were. There are, however, some early and clear indicators.

In the eighteenth century, there was an incidental but rich humor, again, where it wasn't supposed to be—in the soberly delivered criticism of the period. (There is no better example than James Beattie's "Essay on Laughter and Ludicruous Composition.") In addition to the criticism of and about eighteenth-century comic literature, writers like Laurence Sterne, Francis Hutcheson, and George Colman mixed more benign humors into

the critical stew. Theirs were bland efforts, however, and in the
eighteenth century the time for the benign humorists had not yet
arrived.

The early and mid-nineteenth century saw shifting forms of
humor. It ranges from the marooned and quiet laughs which hang
in the air of Dickens's stories to the lesser and more lively humors of such writers as Theodore Hook and Henry Labouchere.
But in a curious and perversely logical way, as the nineteenth
century gave signs of the harsher realities to come, and as the
Industrial Revolution readied for its Spring, it became apparent
to some writers that a benign humor was needed to act as a "national bulwark against the ever-waiting terrors of lunacy, melancholy and spleen."[42] But the benign humorists of the nineteenth century started at a literary disadvantage as the self-
appointed "custodians of English culture," saw any humor sans
wit as unfit for expression other than journalistic. Many of the
humorists, therefore, were asked, and, indeed, forced to cut
their literary teeth while writing for magazines and journals.
There were, however, those humorists who countered the critical dilemma adroitly, even artfully. In addition to Burnaud's
contribution to *Punch*, E. J. Milliken delighted even the fus-
siest intellectuals with his comic verses about the cockney
bounder, "arry."

The literature of the humorists employed an "unresponsive"
(to the times) language that did not fit into tight dogma and tidy
literary classifications—classifications that were, after all,
developed from and for literature using more established and
acceptable languages. To some late nineteenth-century critics,
one of the more heinous crimes committed by the benign humorists was the disregard their "wispy-literature" had for the
tough tenor and low notes of a distinctly unmusical age. It was a
quick step and a faulty syllogism away for worried critics to conclude that if literature were "unreal" ("unresponsive") it was
undeserving of serious consideration. Thus many critics saw
(and continue to see) the "nonsense" language of such a writer
as Carroll as an annihilation—no matter how artful—of linguistic and literary truisms the critics held to be sacrosanct and
more enduring than the crown jewels. The late nineteenth- and

early twentieth-century critics were unwilling and, perhaps, unable to accept alternative languages and the attendant new ways necessary to recognize and analyze the "new languages." The critics were sure that this literature was nothing more than a lark-on-the-wing.

For many of the more benign humorists, there were the literary seductions of "serious literature" and the realities of economic security offered by Fleet Street magazines and newspapers to consider. The lures of critical respectability and economic security proved to be heady and convincing, and those writers who were stopped short of literary fulfillment in the sense of fully developing the skills of the more benign humorists, include E. V. Knox (Evoe), Harry Graham, Marjorie Riddell ("Two's Company"), H. F. Ellis, W. Pett Ridge, Edward Bradley, W. A. Darlington, Owen Rutter, Will Scott, Crosbie Garstin, Derwent Miall, Selwyn Jepson, Harry Leon Wilson ("Ruggles of Red Gap"), W. H. Townend, and Morley Roberts. Many of these skin-deep humorists acquiesced to magazine editors who, due to the binary gods of circulation and advertising, addressed the issues of contemporary life in England. As a result, the humorist was asked to write flashy, contemporary, and remunerative columns and pieces which, in retrospect, seem brilliant only on journalistic palettes.

The nineteenth-century writer most responsible for developing and bringing artistry to the milieu of benign humor was Lewis Carroll. Ironically, 1900 saw Lewis Carroll's literary reputation much in doubt as his literary legacy was uncertain at best. By the twentieth century, his Alice stories seemed ethereal, even effeminate to some critics and, consequently, not considered useful as a tool by which to counter and combat the coiling muscles of an industrial age which recognized strength in machines rather than in art. But Carroll provided the opening into which such writers as A. A. Milne, Kenneth Grahame, Walter de la Mare, Beatrix Potter, and P. G. Wodehouse would rush. Theirs was to be an "alternative literature" which was more than an exercise in "vamping." Unexpectedly and unnoticed, it encouraged different and, to some, "heretical," approaches to literary study other than historical, heuristic, and philological methodologies. By the

beginning of the twentieth century fewer readers would dismiss
the "alternative literature" out of hand. In fact, a small number
of critics and readers suspected that, perhaps, it wasn't fatuous
to wonder whether "The Inane, the Absolute and the Eternal
weren't all one thing."[43]

Not all the benign humorists would stay silent and mute in the
face of critical broadsides. Alan Alexander Milne, for example,
responds to the critical disdain meeting his literature by writing, "The fact that in modern light verse the author does all the
hard work, and that in modern *serious* verse, he leaves it all
to the reader, is a trade secret unknown to a public which still
supposes that *Macbeth* is a 'bigger-performance' than *A Mid-
summer's Night Dream.*"[44] J. B. Priestley, like Belloc opted
for "more literary" forms, those in the favor of the critics.
Priestley, who calls the humorists "those with perfect vision out
a small window. . . ." should have understood their plight since
after writing the overwhelmingly successful *The Good Com-
panions,* he has seen his literary reputation fluctuate and drop
off in almost direct measure to the popular success of the book,
which one confused critic called, "a novel with Dickensian
shape."[45]

By the twentieth century, there were humorists less successful
than Milne, Wodehouse, Grahame and de la Mare, who lacked the
vision and grasp of the "new language" needed to communicate
the new milieu. But this is not to say that Thomas Anstey Guthrie's *Vice-Versa* and *Three Men In a Boat* are not artful.
Indeed, there is nothing limp about H. H. Munro's dry and slightly droll "Saki-isms." J. B. Morton's "Mr. Thrake" stories are
delightful but somewhat less accomplished than the others. Other
significant works which play at the periphery of benign humor
include Lord Dunsany's *The Tortoise and the Hare,* A. E. Cop-
pard's *Willie Waugh,* Daisy Ashford's *The Young Visitors,*
Anthony Armstrong's *Punchamania,* and John Struther's rather
Proustian humor entitled *The Eve of the Shoot.*

The works of the more accomplished humorists, however, promised more. In fact, their writing promised to *deal with* the twentieth
century if only the critics would lay their theories in moth balls
and if only the readers of "light literature" would learn to read
all over again.

3.
England's Benign Humorists

The message of benign-humor does not lie in societal comment nor does it subscribe to the literary proposition that "humor is best expressed in wit." The benign humorists always knew that the literary expression of wit was little more than vapidity disguised as chic banter and badinage.

The literature of benign humor was conceived by writers who deliberately confronted the steel and surge of the late nineteenth and early twentieth century and countered them with "dilly thoughts" wrapped in roses and clouds. The benign humorists materialized into language, alternative worlds, and beings they were content to invest with pristine innocence and uncomplicated grace. This "new humor" was the simple realization by a few writers that the true function of humor was not, as the wits believed, to badger, prod, or even exhilarate the reader with double-entendres, both rhetorical and philosophical. The benign humorists seemed only to want to "help a chap out." Although their literature bespeaks a world constantly antic and in the hay of things, the benign humorists had to endure the absurdity and bruise of the late nineteenth and early twentieth centuries. The humorists, however, replied with a literature that remains ready to carry on in a world rather pitted and fallen.

Benign humor is a literature of absolutes. It is a literature, however, which intuits what it can't see and then reports the vision whole. The benign humorists liked easy definitions, and they

believed that what was not part of their crafted and benign literary worlds had to be elements antithetical to their world-in-language, thus manifestly ignorant and malignant. The major benign humorists of the mid- and late nineteenth and early twentieth centuries in England fall into four specific categories.
These are:

1. Benign humorist as writer of *nonsense language and literature.*
2. Benign humorist as writer of *children's literature.*
3. Benign humorist as *fantasist* and *"beast-fabulist."*
4. Benign humorist as *historian* and *choreographer of fairy lands.*

The significant writers of nonsense literature are Lewis Carroll and Edward Lear. Before dealing with their specific works, however, it is necessary to consider the all too frequent attempts to define nonsense literature.

Literary Confusion over Nonsense

For some, nonsense literature, especially the works of Lewis Carroll, is an expression of the perfect "logic of illogic."[46] Elizabeth Sewall, in the seminal *Field of Nonsense,* makes the same point Michael Holquist makes in his 1969 essay "What Is a Boojum." Both Holquist and Sewall agree that nonsense language and literature are, in reality, quite separate from linguistic chaos and literary disorder. Actually, nonsense language in the literature of the humorists is a highly systematized exercise and expression of newborn linguistics and spilled logic. The problem in comprehending the language of nonsense literature is tied to its disdain of existing grammar and vocabularies and to the disfunction of metaphor encouraged by both Lewis Carroll and Edward

Lear. It is wrong to conclude, however, that nonsense literature is metaphorless.

Nonsense language and its expression in the literature of such nonsense humorists as Carroll and Lear has metaphor *only* *within* the specific language of *nonsense literature*. It cannot be processed, metaphorically, outside of the literature. Thus, within the language of "Jabberwocky," "frumious" means in relation to "Bandersnatch." Outside of Jabberwocky, "frumious" is just eight letters. Thus, each word in nonsense language is "to be one and one and one."[47] In fact, it is more appropriate to conclude that nonsense language hardly *means* at all. It simply is.

Lewis Carroll As Nonsense Humorist

Lewis Carroll is the most accomplished writer of nonsense literature. Carroll, Oxford don, discreet infantasist, and infatuated dreamer of human equations written in toadstools and tarts, created a literature for all ages with his dreaming Alice stories, *Alice in Wonderland* and *Through the Looking Glass*. The stories are inescapably tense but still offer the assurance that rivers and swans will prevail over the unfortunate criticism from *without* which continues to suck at the Alice stories. Lewis Carroll crafts, out of spirits and tensions, stories which work themselves out in illogical, but strangely mathematical ways. Carroll pokes and breaks the heart of traditional patterns of communications as he sets new patterns of an uncommunicative communication into motion. The stories, as a result, seem swarmy and even linguistically aberrant as they deploy strange juxtapositions of language into a *nowhere* that is *everywhere*. Carroll's language—his literature—survives Victorian memories and the play in doilies and drapes of nineteenth-century literature and public disfavor. His *Alice* stories still will not bend and blow away with the times, as the Oxford don unties the connections between words and thoughts, flooding both into a timeless space. He was, perhaps, unaware that some might equate "timeless" with "meaningless." Carroll, however, suspected that language and literature received their power from meaninglessness.

Carroll knew the English. He knew they liked their literature light and their verses highly musical. In her essay "Lewis Carroll and T. S. Eliot as Nonsense Poets," Elizabeth Sewall indicates the predilection of many writers of light English literature to turn material into "simple music," a necessity since "the English prefer their poetry pure." She further points to the literary mannerism by which many English writers "struggle" to convert language "into symbolic language or music."[48] Indeed, Carroll's "Alice" stories have all the lazy scan and edge of a pastoral symphony. But Carroll's music means nothing outside the orchestration of his own stories. (In this regard, one suspects that Carroll might have been pleased with composer-conductor Leonard Bernstein's Charles Eliot Norton Lecture series in which Bernstein indicated a musical-linguistic-semiology which means only in terms of notes, movements, et al. In the lectures, Bernstein questions the appropriateness of applying musical signs to extramusical considerations, for example, why do notes in a low register traditionally stand as metaphor for storminess, brooding, etc.)

Carroll's use of language demanded from him a certain literary asceticism which first limits and then eliminates consideration of *other* language. This is more than a matter of will, however, as Carroll opts to limit himself to a language that denies duplication. Such redundancy, after all, exhausts itself in metaphorical analyses and structurally defined discussions. By giving his language no license to gambol about, however, Lewis Carroll uses an extra-literary language which threatens to exhaust itself in a constant search for originality. His books, chapters, paragraphs, sentences, and words — according to his own concept of iconic language — have about them a once-in-a-lifetime quality.

Nowhere in Lewis Carroll's work, of course, is there a better example of the literature of nonsense that that implicit in the verse "Jabberwocky" which appears in *Through the Looking Glass.* Within the strange ambience of "Jabberwocky," attempts are made to decode the poem, no matter how delightfully uninformed. John Ciardi, for example, attempts to "dope-out" the sense of it all without deciding whether "frumious" means "furious" or "gloomious." Ciardi, of course, might well ask if "Bander-snatch" doesn't after all, mean a "person who snatches at banter."[49]

Indeed, it is difficult to gather certainties from a literature which has all the territorial similitude of dream and wish. It is important, however, to show the possible variations when trans-lating "Jabberwocky." Thus, while for Eric Partridge, the word "frumious" suggests a blend of "frumpish" and "gloomy," it is possible to conjecture that "frumious" means fussy and ruinous while "brillig" means brilliant and slick. In fact, "slithy" means slimy and sneaky, "gimble" means gambol and nimble, while "mimsy" might combine the mimetic and sissified. "Bor-ogroves" means quite simply, borrowed-groves, while "mome" speaks to solemnity and moment. "Outgrabe" means reaching and grasping, while the "jubjub" is either a pelican or a cuckoo (although the former was already an endangered species around Oxford in the nineteenth century). "Vorpal" seems a blend of vortex and torporous, while "manxome" is the epitome of manic dexterity. The "tumtum tree" is either delicious or hollow or, paradoxically, both; the "uffish" thought is characteristic of those dulled but uppity. In "Jabberwocky" something comes whistling and whispering through the woods or, as Carroll puts it, "wiffling." The "tulgey woods" are turgid and bulging, and "burbles" combine bubbling and gulping. The "snicker-snack" is clean, quick, crisp, and cutting. After galloping and gulping— "galumphing"—the "beamish" boy is bright and sensuous as the "frabjous" day (fabulous and joyous) recommends a hurrah and a hooray or, even a "callooh" and "callay."

Carroll, with "Jabberwocky," prefigured a linguistic theory which was not to be expressed until the twentieth century. In "Jabberwocky," and to a lesser degree in the prose of the "Alice" stories, Carroll makes use of what logician Charles Peirce labelled "iconic signs." (Simply stated, an "iconic sign" (or word) is a sign that represents its object by its similarity to it, rather than by and through some metaphorical inference.) Iconic signs abound in the Alice stories. Even the human senses seem aberrant and quite iconic, and in *Alice in Wonderland*

Alice drinks from a bottle and finds it "very nice," with a taste
that "[has] a sort of mixed flavour of cherry-tart, custard,
pineapple, roast turkey, taffy and hot-buttered toast. . . ."[50]
Carroll, however, invests his iconic signs with dimensions
fraught with an inter alia essence. And in *Alice in Wonderland*
Alice tries to fancy what the flame of a candle looks like after it
is blown out, for, true to the substitution of iconic sign for indexi-
cal memory, Alice could not "remember having seen such a
thing."[51] Carroll's iconic language, of course, seems to masquerade as confusion. But such designated "confusion" should
serve only to make the careful reader and the discreet scholar
"curiouser" and "curiouser."

To write "perfect nonsense" is, by its very nature, exhausting
and quite limiting. So, perhaps, Carroll can be forgiven a typographical affectation by which he stretches words to insure the
iconic integrity of *Alice in Wonderland*. Thus, while her new
friend the mouse speaks to her, Alice's preoccupation and dis-
interest in the rodent's rhetoric is implied by Carroll's snaking her
meandering interpretation of what the mouse says, lazily, dreamily
and artfully down the page.

In the *Alice* books there are iconic and even technological
implausibilities. There is in fact, something correctly misplaced
and surreal about the verse;

> Twinkle, twinkle, little bat!
> How I wonder what you're at!
> Up above the world you fly,
> Like a tea-tray in the sky.
> Twinkle, twinkle-[52]

It is more than precious discourse to talk about the zoological
iconicity in *Alice in Wonderland* when Alice and the Duchess
talk of the Flamingo.

> "He might bite," Alice cautiously replied . . .
> "Very true," said the Duchess: "flamingos and
> mustard both bite. And the moral of that is 'Birds
> of a feather flock together.' "
> "Only mustard isn't a bird," Alice remarked.
> "Right as usual," said the Duchess, "What a clear
> way you have of putting things!"
> "It's a mineral, I think," said Alice."[53]

With the twentieth-century success of Carroll's *Alice* books has come an academic theory which views the mathematician as the nineteenth-century's archetypal dadaist. Such a theory, however, obfuscates essential points about nonsense humor and dadaism. Dada art in the twentieth century was essentially *destructive*. Its sole raison d'etre was to obscure, thus destroy, existing art forms and the ways in which they communicated. Nonsense literature, on the other hand, was conceived from, and *constructed* on, new languages. Walter Sorrel is correct when he concludes that nonsense literature is "superior" to dadaism in that "it is nonsense that makes sense as nonsense."[54] Inherent in nonsense language and literature is the implication of on-goingness, the vitality of continuance, and the possibility of birth. There is, for example, brimming hopefulness in Alice's question, "How can I know what I think till I see what I say?"

For some, Lewis Carroll's *Alice* books and their "organized-chaotic language" were written according to strict rules of "gamesmanship." Sewell, one of the more precise scholars of Lewis Carroll has written, ". . . each game . . . is an enclosed whole with its own rigid laws which cannot be questioned within the game itself." She continues, once "inside the system which is the game, you bind yourself by that system of laws and so incidentally attain the particular sense of freedom which [it] has to offer."[55] Although she has written widely and most sensibly about the benign humorists, Sewall misses the point somewhat when she theorizes that the literature (the "game") cannot be questioned from inside. It is only from within Carroll's *Alice* books—with an understanding that the *oeuvre* will not be understood by applying literary technique and linguistic methodologies from *without*—that the writer and his works yield anything of a remunerative or theoretical value. In addition, it seems that anyone who would tell his printer to change "can't" to the more accurate "ca'n't," as Carroll did, had something more than "gamesmanship" in mind.

The Nonsense of Edward Lear

Edward Lear's nonsense literature is significantly different from that of Lewis Carroll. Where the reader is never quite sure if Carroll wants to amuse or spook, the reader of Edward Lear's nonsense verse and limericks is certain that the writer wants desperately to be nothing else but humorous. Unlike Carroll's language, which seems to spring from the voids of fantasy, Lear's language is earthly, studied, and *deliberately* nonsensical. Where Carroll's language and words add up to just what they are, Lear's words and verses are too silly and skittish to stand for any addition. The linguistic force and literary quality of Lear's lines depend on the reader's predisposition toward the literature at the moment the words are being read and experienced. So with Lear, the nonsense of his verses is tied to the reading process and the gratification the process gives the individual reader. It is to Lear's credit as a tactician that the apprehension of his verses seems so consistent and critically informed.

In a curious way, Lear's nonsense verses are both more and less nonsensical than Lewis Carroll's "Alice" stories. They are *less* nonsensical in that Lear wrote them according to a careful design which makes their effect predictable and, in a crueler, literary way, tiresome. But, at the same time, Lear's verses are *more* nonsensical in that Lear mines so much nonsense through a predictable and simple selection of the "wrong word" for the "right place." And what is truly nonsensical about such a simplistic approach is that one wonders why Lear would want to do *just that*. But Lear is a successful nonsensist and while his verses lack a certain complexity and artistry, they make up for it with cunning sound and delightfully misplaced logic.

Teapots and Quails is quintessential Lear with four-line verses the writer assiduously, if whimsically, complemented with bizzare illustrations no less pleasing and humorous than the verses themselves. But unlike the enduring quality of the *Alice* books, Lear's verses trail off, each verse offering one smile. Even within one smile, however, there can be the unexpected. In

Mitres and beams,
Thimbles and Creams,
Set him a screaming
and hark! how he screams!

the use of "cream" in the plural ("Creams") is, for an instant, unexpected. The plural does, of course, allow the verse to move —a flow predictably interrupted by that curious predilection of the nineteenth- and twentieth-century benign humorists to overuse the exclamation point. Lear, however, was conscious of writing lines that had "perfick-scan" and built-in lilt. But frequently and delightfully the continuity of his verse is shattered by words and lines that are incongruent and seemingly not deliberate. For example, the line "Ribands and Pigs, Helmets and Figs," seems harsh and inappropriately severe when viewed after its accompanying line, "Tadpoles and Tops, Teacups and Mops."[57]

Lear is an acknowledged master of those rhetorical and literary devices used so often by humorists who remained deft and unembarrassed when reaching into their bag of tricks. And in

> Herons and Sweeps,
> Turbans and Sheeps,
> Set him a weeping
> and see how he weeps!

Lear again uses a bogus plural — "sheeps."[58] But Lear, more conscious of the *motion* of benign humor than others adds the plural to a verb (sweep) and sweeps it into a noun ("Sweeps"). Such deliberate use of the grammatically incorrect word or expression has long been a literary staple of the benign humorists. Lear also makes comic use of the incongruity and unpredictability of key words; with one foot in the Surrey meadows and the other in Constantinople, he writes:

> Sofas and bees,
> Camels and Keys,
> Set him a sneezing
> And see how he'll sneeze![59]

Lear's unpredictability, however, does not always work, as he frequently mixes an innocent line with one less benign, even malignant. For example, the line "Cutlets and eyes" is too graphic and unpleasant when followed with "Swallows and Pies." In the lines "Eagles and pears, Slippers and Bears," the gentle sweep

of the second line seems inappropriate when following "Eagles."
Indeed, the first line seems incongruous and threatening. Lear is
more successful when being most innocuous and playful. There
is nothing but elegant innocence in

> Wafers and Bears,
> Ladders and Squares,
> Set him a staring,
> and see how he stares![60]

Like most of the benign humorists, Lear is canny when it
comes to sensing the benignity and innocence in the very letters
of a word. He must have understood completely, for example, why
a fish named "trout" has always been attractive and heroic in
English literature. Lear knows his fish and romances them well,
if in a most unromantic verse. Indeed, there is civility in

> Thistles and Moles,
> Crumpets and Soles,
> Set it a rolling
> And see how it rolls![61]

Lear uses words for their immanent qualities, and their meaning
in the scheme of his verses is surprisingly independent of their
positioning in the lines. This is a notable achievement for a humorist who relies so heavily on the motion and sound in four,
short-lines. Thus, one is curiously struck by "custards" in

> Watches and Oaks,
> Custards and Cloaks,
> Set him a poking
> and see how he pokes![62]

Many of Lear's verses succeed and fail according to the "in-
synchness" or "out-of-synchness" of their four lines. The
reader, for example, does not question Lear's "in-synch" verses
such as

> Hurdles and Mumps,
> Poodles and pumps,
> Set it a jumping
> And see how he jumps![63]

But there is something jarring and "out-of-synch" in

> Volumes and Pigs
> Razors and Figs,
> Set him a jigging
> and see how he jigs![64]

The reader wonders what "Razors" is doing in the verse. Considering the benign uniformity of most of Lear's verses, one wonders if the somewhat diabolical "Razors" doesn't have something to do with that person whom Lear "set . . .a jigging."

Lear's verses, of course, are peculiarly English. The Learian reader should be familiar with English speech patterns and habits. To appreciate the perfect rhyme in Lear's verses, the reader must shed what Anthony Burgess calls "Ameriglish" and must read in "Britglish" if wanting to get the most out of

> Gruel and prawns,
> Bracelets and Thorns,
> Set him a yawning
> and see how he yawns![65]

There is nothing typically English, however, about Lear's infrequent, euphoric inconsistencies. And where it is easy to hear the smoothness and even motion in "Trumpets and Guns, beetles and buns," it is more difficult to get a smooth read with "Saucers and Tops, Lobsters and Mops."[66] For Lear, it is a "bad lob."

In the *Limericks* Lear raises the artistry of his nonsense literature to its highest level. Not the least indication of the limerick's artistry is the realization that they are humorous in ways perhaps unintentional. Indeed, there is something discursive yet highly humorous in

> There was an old person of Brussels,
> Who Lived upon Brandy and Mussels.
> When he rushed through the town, he knocked most
>   people down
> Which distressed all the people of Brussels.[67]

The limerick, besides being invested with the abstractions of absurdity, wrings humor from the mere repetition of a word. Consequently, the limerick seems almost careless as Lear hap-

pens upon "Mussels" which he rhymes with the first "Brussels."
Lear, however, is not concerned with finding another word to
rhyme with "Brussels" or "Mussels." To be sure, Lear is too
much the careful craftsman to opt out of rhyme-scheme for reasons of laziness and artless accommodation. Indeed, what seems a
cavalier selection of words never fails to add puzzle and enigma
to Lear's verses. For example, an innocuous limerick turns ambiguous with the appearance of the word "persistent" in

> There was an old man of the hills,
> Who lived upon Syrup of Squills;
> Which he drank all night long, to the sound of a gong
> That persistent old man of the hills.[68]

And it is the "susceptible" reader who is seduced into seeing
nothing in

> There was an old man of Girgenti,
> Who lived in profusion and plenty;
> He lay on two chairs, and ate thousands of pears,
> That susceptible man of Girgenti.[69]

Critical Limitations

Appropriately enough, there continues to be much confusion
about such consummate writers of benign nonsense as Lewis
Carroll and Edward Lear. This, of course, is as it should be. It
is the too easily misled reader of the literature, however, who
dismisses out of hand the literature of writers who designed and
crafted the seemingly undesignable and craftless. The critical
problem for such writers as Carroll and Lear is implicit in the
word "nonsense." (The Oxford English Dictionary offers little
in the way of clarification as it lists the following definitions for
the word "nonsense": 1—that which is not sense; spoken or written
words which make no sense or convey absurd ideas, also absurd

action; 2—absurdity, nonsensicalness; 3—unsubstantial or worthless
stuff or things; 4—A meaning that makes no sense.)

The nineteenth- and twentieth-century confusion over the *purposely confused* continues. Undeniably, nonsense literature such
as Lewis Carroll's *Alice* books and Lear's frequently painful
and humble verses and limericks receives its definition as "nonsense" or "absurdist literature," not only from the writing itself, but also as a result of the considerable, if inconsiderate,
criticism attending the literature. Moreover, it is clear that
present and future critics must consider Lewis Carroll's *Alice*
books and Lear's verses and limericks as literature partially
subverted by the dimensionless discourse of those who have felt
it incumbent upon them to add light where none was asked.

Any reading of the literature of Lewis Carroll and Edward
Lear, however, denies the appropriateness of the *The Oxford
English Dictionary*'s third definition — "unsubstantial and
worthless stuff or things." A simple exercise in semantics, of
course, is all that is needed to dispel the inaccuracy of such definitions of nonsense literature as "unsubstantial or worthless."
It is clear, for example, that for *something* to prove substantial, it need only exhibit a full meaning and demonstrate a certain significance *within its own context, milieu, genre.* If it
demonstrates less "weight"—meaning and significance—than
some like entity extrinsic in form and time, there is still no reason to deem it unsubstantial or worthless. Such perverse and
twisted relativism is quite meaningless. So where William Blake
in "Infant Joy" made a clear break with the fashionable language" of the eighteenth century with such benign verse as

> I have no name
> I am but two days old.
> What should I call thee?
> "I happy am,
> Joy is my name."
> Sweet joy befall thee![70]

and was bitterly criticized for what appeared to be a new and
artless "simplicity," Lewis Carroll and Edward Lear have been
denied their literary due by those who insist upon comparing the

"seemingly simple" works of the two benign humorists to writings from dissimilar comic veins.

The word "simple" is key when assessing the literature of Carroll and Lear. Too often the "simplicity" of a Learian verse is equated in its "simplicity" with such words as "banal" and "inane." But the concept of simplicity (when applied to nonsense literature) means *that which is not combined with anything else.* Indeed, the nonsense literature of Carroll and Lear is *not* combinable with language and meaning extrinsic to the genre of nonsense literature.

When *doing criticism* of Carroll and Lear, the critical mind must remain free of dated theory. Contemporaneous, orderly and meticulous criticism bodes well for the rather inviolable literature of such benign nonsensists as Carroll and Lear—writers who encouraged few questions from those without.

The difficulty in critiquing the literature of Carroll and Lear, however, should not indicate a moratorium on critical comment which addresses the two benign humorists. Critical propriety must intervene before the critic falls to the tugs and academic pulls of sophistic comparison and pedantic conclusion. Thus it is appropriate to conclude that Carroll is being *somewhat* surreal when writing about "twinkling bats" and "flying tea-sets" on the glide. It is inappropriate, however, to determine critically if Lewis Carroll's surrealism is equal in artistry to the designing surrealists. In the same way, of course, it is significant to note that there is something rather sinister about "Razors and Figs," something mustard-like and deep-going in "Gruel and prawns," without comparing Edward Lear's verses and limericks to English Gaslightisms and the scarlet Dickensian humours weltering in the darker parts of a rather un-Learian and grim London. There is nothing gothic or romantic about Carroll's boats slipping away and listing about water which breezes and greens beneath its young crew—there is only something quite Carrollian. And while rearranged hearts and whispering dresses may have meaning in terms of small spites, moveable hearts, and fluttering fabric, it is the careless reader of the literature who tries to find the mean and eerie. It hardly matters at all that there is something worried but thunderously unromantic about

Edward Lear's beams, creams, and softened screams. And although Lear mixes "Turbans" and "Sheeps," the reader need not question the geographic inaccuracy of having "Turbans" surrounded by "Sheeps." Lear can coin "numbrella," but the well-advised reader should not mind theories about negated bumbershoots and should not assume Learian intent beyond rhyme reaching.

While Lewis Carroll's literature remains balanced in the brillig of equations purposely slipped out of form, Lear's verses continue to twist on tips of "oyster-clippers." Lear, of course, would merely smile at those who concluded "strange sea-food," "ineffectual scissors." Indeed, the benign literature of Lewis Carroll and Edward Lear asks to be left alone. Ironically, the most effective and appropriate way for the critics to leave the literature alone is to know when to stop discussing it.

4.
Benign Humorists of Children's Literature

The major writers of children's literature among the benign humorists are A. A. Milne, Beatrix Potter, and, curiously enough, P. G. Wodehouse. It is still unclear, however, as to the proper way to proceed when attempting to define "children's literature." For example, is it for children five- to ten-years old, or for children ten to sixteen, or is it for any reader who acts "childlike" or any reader who "has the mind of a child"? It seems clear and fair to conclude that "children's literature" just happens to be a literature which has been written for "smallish" people but can be enjoyed by anyone. A. A. Milne's Pooh stories have this broad appeal even though Pooh's world gives more of itself to young readers who, like Pooh and his animal friends, break their bones easily only to see them quickly knit for the next "frumptious day."

The Pooh Stories of A. A. Milne

Where A. A. Milne's Pooh stories are robust and careless as his animals career and bump delightfully off each other, the animals in Beatrix Potter's stories seem to look sumptuously for opportunity in every bush as they stalk quietly about England's Lake District. Each of Potter's stories is a solitaire; each a slight tale framed by the golden glow of tame illustrations. Like those of Milne, Potter's stories are charmingly frail, but unlike the Pooh books, Potter's stories seem to have a teardrop at the center of each laugh. In each story there is a melancholy shift—not much more than a slight rustling in the leaves as the rabbits and squirrels pal about in work and play until their resources of cheer are exhausted by the day. And while they know that night can mean broken hearts, Potter's animals know fourteen and sixteen hours of sunlight. Potter's illustrations deny harsher realities as each autumn links to spring and then back to autumn in a sure and lazy cycle of unthreatening seasons which skip over the bald intrusions of blunt summers and edged winters.

Potter and Milne's stories offer an adventurous but curiously simplistic literature to young readers, while, at the same time, they offer something unstatable to adult readers from whom they demand more. It is not the fault of Potter and Milne, after all, if most "adult readers" have been conditioned to dismiss any literature that can be understood and enjoyed by sons and daughters. It is also not the fault of the "adult reader" who has been asked by the nineteenth and twentieth century to juggle jade and machines. For the young reader the Pooh stories and Potter's animal tales are *reality* being played out in the woods in the next state or county. The younger reader does not apprehend the stories as fantasy or fanciful renderings of dreams. For the adult reader children's literature seems hopelessly "unreal," as the adult suspects that there's more to life than barking trees and things in threes that actually don't make a crowd.

In the Pooh stories, A. A. Milne affects a simple enough and quite literary modus-operandi as he takes and emphasizes a dominant characteristic in each of the animals. He amusingly but graciously highlights Pooh's considerable appetite, Owl's pedantry, Piglet's timidity, and Tigger's unabashed energy. To his Edenic woods, Milne also adds the misanthropic Eeyore, a sensitive Christopher Robin (Milne's son's alter ego) an innocuous Kanga and Roo, a deliberately absent Heffalump, and various tiger cats and fluttering and scurrying items in feather and fur. Milne, conscious of never disturbing the fragile spirit and dignity of animals in a twentieth century which promised them but a plow and a cage, does not let the forest terrorize its travellers, and as a result the forest animals are "kinder than the kindest men...".[71] In the stories even the air is enchanted as Milne turns Christopher Robin's whistles into incantations. It is in this ariel paradise where Milne places his pal-about animals who "... do not teach the child's mind, but educate his heart."[72]

Milne, like Carroll, Lear, and to some extent Wodehouse, was aware of the benign humorist's need for iconic language. Thus when the father in *Winnie the Pooh* tells his son (Milne at the beginning of the story talking to his son) that Edward the Pooh Bear lives in a forest "under the name of Sanders," Christopher Robin, with a mind iconically pristine and uncluttered by history, (experience *qua* metaphor), responds quite correctly, "What does under the name mean?"

With the Pooh books, Milne indulges, as Carroll had before him, the English humorist's predilection for musical and lyrical prose and verse. Milne's music is resplendent in the use of sound-blending — words which blend ("blendwords") so well that they call for orchestration. Thus, even the title *Winnie the Pooh* becomes even more melodically, "winnietherpooh, " while a pinched Christopher Robin becomes "christopherowrobin." Frequently, Milne's animals hang about the "Winnie the Pooh Tree" or the "winniethepoohtree." At the bear's house is a door jam, a knocker ("doorjamknocker") and a bell-pull ("bellpull"). There is also Christopher Robin's sign which reads "North Pole, Discovered by Pooh, Pooh found it!" The final notes are clear, if not "pooh-found."

Milne keeps his melodies sweet and delicate, smallish and rare. Even Pooh's verses and songs are in "tra-la-la's," and "rum-tum-tiddles," as the "rollish-bear" marks the air with staffs and measures. Milne also shows the benign-humorist's skill at creating melody out of prose written in short words with small portent. For example,

> One day when the sun had come back over the forest, bringing with it the scent of may, and all the streams of the forest were tinkling happily to find themselves their own pretty shape

again, and the little pools lay dreaming of the life they had
seen and the big things they had done, and in the warmth and
quiet of the Forest, the cuckoo was trying over his voice
carefully and listening to see if he liked it, and wood pigeons
were complaining gently to themselves in their lazy comfortable way that it was the other fellow's fault, but it didn't
matter very much; on such a day as this, Christopher Robin
whistled in a special way he had, and Owl came flying out of
the Hundred Acre Wood to see what was wanted.[73]

Milne, with this passage, shows his affection for music played in
easy notes and in a lowing and small register. It is not a typographical ruse which sees the month of "may" in lower case. The passage
has a Delian flow as the cuckoo practices quietly while pools "lay
dreaming" and the wood pigeons complain in a "lazy and comfortable way."

Milne, a frustrated philosopher, liked to express himself syllogistically; in his children's literature, Pooh is the ready logician.
When the bruin hears "buzzing" noises in a tree, he offers that the
only reason for *any* buzzing noise is "because you're a bee."
Pooh concludes that the only reason for being a bee is "to make
honey." He further concludes that "the only reason for making
honey is so as I can eat it."[74] When Pooh sees a hole in the bank of
the river he says: "If I know anything about anything, that hole
means Rabbit . . . and Rabbit means company, and Company
means Food and Listening-to me-humming."[75] The logic is in-
cisively deductive. For example, when Christopher Robin wonders
how he and Pooh are ever to recognize the North Pole, he con-
jectures "I suppose it's just a pole stuck in the ground." To which
Rabbit replies, "sure . . . a pole . . . because of calling it a pole
and if it's a pole, well, I should think it would be sticking in the
ground, shouldn't you, because there'd be nowhere else to stick
it?"[76]

Milne's animals are conscious of never wanting to hurt fellow-
fur. Frequently Pooh will go to deferential length not to appear
forward or aggressive. Thus, desperately wanting a balloon, Pooh
asks, "I wonder if Christopher Robin has such a thing as a balloon
about him? I just said it to myself thinking of balloons and wondering."[77] Milne's animals are delightfully self-conscious as well.

The resourceful Pooh, for example, counters his attractive ignorance with various face-saving techniques. And when Pooh is asked if his being quiet means that he doesn't have an answer to a problem that he had led others to believe he "could handle," he answers, "N-no . . . just resting and thinking and humming to myself."⁷⁸ When given a letter which he refuses to admit he cannot read, Pooh tells the others that he cannot read it ". . . owing to having got some water in my eyes." Piglet is another of Milne's great face-savers, and after being so frightened that he jumps high into the air, in order to show that he hadn't been frightened at all, Piglet continues to jump "up and down once or twice in an exercising sort of way."⁷⁹

Unlike the more assertive use of nonsense language by Carroll and Lear, Milne uses familiar words in muddled constructions. For example, when Piglet asks a mysterious acting Pooh, "Tracking what?" Pooh answers, "That's just what I ask myself, What?" to which Piglet wryly responds, "What do you think you'll answer?" ⁸⁰ And when Eeyore is asked by the Pooh Bear *how* he is feeling, the donkey answers, "Not very how, I don't seem to have felt at all how for a long time."⁸¹ Milne indulges in phonetic playfulness as well, and when Owl says, "Customary Procedure" to Pooh, the bear's mistranslation becomes "Crustimony Proseedcake." When Owl says "Issue" to the bear, Pooh inexplicably turns it, not to "Tissue," but one step more into "sneeze." Milne also has a deft feel for ludicrous situations and he brings them easily to their punning conclusions. So Owl is chastised for making off with Eeyore's tail as Pooh informs the pedantic Owl that the donkey was "fond of it," indeed, quite "attached to it."⁸²

Milne's "Pooh" stories, however, are products of something more than easy device and rhetorical gymnastics. The careful "adult" reader can appreciate Milne's unexpected euphorias and well-placed ecstasies. The ecstasy of returned love in Milne's stories is spellbinding, if not heartbreaking, as even the most cynical reader is touched when Christopher Robin looks at his friend the Pooh-bear with damp and glistening eyes and blurts out, "Oh! Bear! How I do love you!" Pooh, of course, answers, "So do I."⁸³ The Pooh tales have an undeniable tenderness which is only slightly toughened by an infrequent sense of fear and brooding. When Christopher Robin loses his friend Pooh, he cries to the darkness, "Pooh, oh Pooh, where are you." A relieved bear hears the cry and nonchalantly answers, "Here I am." But blase detachment does not carry in Milne's stories, and both Christopher Robin and Pooh rush into each other's arms as their eyes catch at their tears and their hands and paws clutch for security.

Milne has proved that older and larger appetites can be satisfied as even the "adult" reader is satiated on small cheers as Pooh winningly proclaims, "Nobody can be uncheered with a *balloon*."[84] Each moment in the Pooh books rollicks and rolls in green meadows which lose the horizon. But in Milne's meadows and fields "adult" business goes unconducted. "Things" there are small and the stresses of larger, adult lives are absent and unimportant. In these woods, there are no bad spellers, only those who spell in ways that "wobble and get in the wrong places."[85]

Literary critics and scholars always made Milne uneasy and even suspicious as he worried over their assessment of him as a literary underachiever. He did not always ignore the brief lures and satisfactions of counterattack as he has Pooh and his animal friends discuss the aesthetic sophistications professed by those critics who held Milne's art in something less than high esteem. Unexpectedly, Milne, through Pooh, makes essential points about literary aesthetics. For example, Pooh tells his best friend Christopher Robin how he, the supreme cuddle-bear, composes his verses and hums, "I shall sing the first line twice and, perhaps, if I sing it quickly, I shall find myself singing the third and fourth line before I have time to think of them and that will be a good song."[86] The result of such cavalier theorizing, of course, is masterful. And in the song "Sing Ho! For the life of a Bear," Pooh sings

> Sing Ho! for the life of a Bear!
> Sing Ho! for the life of a Bear!
> I don't much mind if it rains or snows,
> 'Cos I've got a lot of honey on my nice new nose,
> I don't much care if it snows or thaws,
> 'Cos I've got a lot of honey on my nice clean paws!
> Sing Ho! for a Bear!
> Sing Ho! for a Pooh!
> And I'll have a little something in an hour or two![87]

Much of the implicit charm of Milne's children's literature can be traced to its direct appeal to the instinct rather than to

the processes of reasoning and intelligence. Pooh hasn't much of
a brain—a reality which insures his never coming to any harm.
Lack of brain in the Pooh stories is equated with the surer power
of nature and primitive intelligence. Milne makes the same
point time and time again, and Piglet offers; "... Owl hasn't
exactly got Brain, but he knows Things."[88] Milne also knew
that sure instincts did not always take care of feelings. He knew
that small hurts can leave big bruises, but Milne allows the hurt
and denies the bruise while the self-deprecating Eeyore sees
himself as rather ineffectual and quite without friends. Eeyore
speaks "I have my friends. Somebody spoke to me only yester-
day."

In his story, *The House at Pooh Corner,* Milne's benign
touch seems less successful than its expression in the simpler
Winnie the Pooh. With *The House at Pooh Corner,* Milne
maintained a surer grip on literary device. As he did in *Winnie
the Pooh,* Milne again makes use of tangled thoughts, the logic
of illogic, deductive reasoning, euphoric-blending, and coined
language.

And so when Pooh peers into Piglet's home and sees that the
porker isn't there, he keeps searching and gazing into the home
"... and the more he looked inside, the more Piglet wasn't
there."[89] In *The House at Pooh Corner,* as he did to a lesser extent in *Winnie the Pooh,* Milne made consummate use of
euphonious blend-words. Examples include "thinking-walk"
(thinkingwalk), "Pooh and Piglet" (poohandpiglet), "master-
shalumseed," and some*thing* called "two-stymes." In *The
House at Pooh Corner,* for example, there appears such words
as "smackeral," "worraworroworra," "skoos-e," "stripy,"
"golollop," "organidized," "sterny," "jagulars," "hooshing,"
"coffy," "squoze," "squch," and "spudge."

The House at Pooh Corner is a more literary and self-
conscious effort. In fact, the story is replete with literary and
critical points which Milne, perhaps feeling too stamped by the
appellation "writer of children's literature," was anxious to
make. Milne, for example, alludes to the importance of prose
music and poetic melody as the poet laureate of the Hundred Acre
Woods, Pooh-bear, tells Piglet of the importance of the over-

used songs. "Poms," explains Pooh, are "put . . . in to make [them] more hummy."⁹⁰ Milne was aware of the stern critics who saw his stories as "rather ridiculous," "arcane," "nothing but fluff." But he also knew that language, left in the mouths and minds of animals and "small people," discouraged and, at least, reduced critical plunder. Pooh bear remarks, for example, "[when] you Think of Things, you find, sometimes, that a Thing which seemed very Thingish inside you is quite different when it gets out into the open and has other people looking at it."⁹¹ Milne had a naturalist's feel for the poetic process, and in *The House at Pooh Corner,* Pooh says ". . . Poetry and Hums aren't things which you get, they're things which get you. And all you can do is to go where they can find you."⁹² Pooh adds, ". . . [and] the best way to write poetry [is] letting things come."⁹³

In *The House at Pooh Corner,* Milne once again has his animals deduce logic and "other things" by logical and simple means. Piglet, therefore, tells Tigger "I thought Tiggers were smaller than that," after which the "stripy cat" replies, "Not the big ones." And when Eeyore is told that Tigger has just come to the Forest, the donkey with perfect wisdom asks "When is he going?"⁹⁵ After Tigger catches a thistle in his paw, Eeyore, not the best of logicians, asks ". . . why bend a perfectly good one?"⁹⁶ The platonic Roo tells Piglet that Tigger can't climb *down* a tree because his tail would naturally get in the way. It is quite clear to Piglet that the word "climb" should not be thought of in terms of descent. Pooh, with the perfect logic of a humanist on the hum, addresses the problem brought about by Tigger's habitual leaping from behind bushes and trees in order to scare the daylights and nightlight out of Rabbit. Pooh suggests his simple solution in a verse.

If Rabbit
was bigger
And fatter
And stronger,
or Bigger
than Tigger,
If Tigger was smaller,

The Tigger's bad habit
of bouncing at Rabbit,
Would matter
No longer
if Rabbit
was taller.[97]

But Piglet reminds Pooh that "Rabbit has Brain." This discourages the bear and diminishes the chances his verse has to
rectify the problem of Tigger's benign bullying, since Pooh-bear
realizes that "Brain" is responsible for Rabbits who "never understand anything."[98] There is about the perfect logic of
Milne's near perfect animal-folk the laze and glow of indolent
sentimentalities. And as Christopher Robin sighs and tells the
bear ". . . what I like doing best is Nothing," Pooh asks "How
do you do nothing?" Christopher Robin, tired from lying in the
sun and picking buttercups, answers, "Well, it's when people
call at you just as you're going off to do it . . ."[99] It is not
the simplest of logics.

In *The House at Pooh Corner,* as in *Winnie the Pooh,*
Milne speaks to the special ecstasies always at the bubble in
the corners of young eyes and constantly being encouraged under
pink cheeks. When analyzing the ecstasies, however, the reader
must deny the inappropriate conclusion. In Milne's stories, even
sexual excitations are pre-pubescent and when Christopher
Robin takes off "his tunic," Piglet narrates ". . . he [Pooh] was
so agog at . . . seeing Christopher Robin's blue braces, . . .
being a little over-excited by them, [he] had to go to bed half an
hour earlier than usual. . . ."[100]

By the end of *The House at Pooh Corner,* however, Milne
seems to have run out of blisses and good cheers. Reality bears
as Milne shows Christopher Robin, who, by the end of the story
is threatened by adolescence, the microcosm of the macrocosm in
the flowing river which slips inexorably beneath a temporal
bridge. Christopher Robin "suddenly knows" that he must leave
the enchanted lands of Pooh and his friends. For Christopher
Robin, knowledge and insight rudely reveal the implausibility of
living a pure, primitive existence free of earthy concerns.   He
learns that the world demands his work and participation. And

if *The House at Pooh Corner* is a less accomplished example of "benign literature," its conclusion, where Christopher Robin cuts the silken and weakened ties to Pooh-land and explains his actions to Pooh who seems to remain loving but unconcerned, gives "light" English literature one of its most moving passages.

The Adventures of Beatrix Potter

Perhaps the major reason why Beatrix Potter's "children's books" do not work as well on the level of benign humor as do Milne's Pooh stories is contained in a single quote from Margaret Lane's book *The Tale of Beatrix Potter,* in which the writer's friend "explains" the reasons for Potter's success (success that finds her books selling into the millions while being translated into several foreign languages). For Lane, the artistry in Potter's stories is in the "high level of execution, founded partly on a naturalist's loving observation of animal life, partly on an imaginative awareness of its character [which] lifts her work into a class of its own among children's books."[101] Indeed, Potter's animal stories (*Tale of Peter Rabbit, The Tailor of Gloucester, Jemima Puddle Duck, Squirrel Nutkin,* et al), unlike those of A. A. Milne, reveal a curious distance between the writer and her material—the lovely animals. As Lane suggests, Potter approaches her animals and "observes" them in an almost clinical way. But even though she seems to be the writer-as-lay-scientist, Beatrix Potter's stories are not dispassionate studies invested with only slight, naturalistic charms. Potter respects what she finds out about her ducks and rabbits, and her writings and illustrations glow with "... family life that goes on in burrows and holes." It is a credit to her artistry that her slim books contain so much love for

... the natural detail of hedge, and ditch and kitchen garden, the revelation of beauty and dewy freshness in the
northern countryside, the homeliness of its farm kitchens,
the cool smell of dairies, the fragrance of baking
days . . .[102]

There is edge but no terror in Potter's kitchens or in the
animal farms where the landscapes are suffused with happy ga-
lores and sugary delights which measure the land and survey the
hearts living on it. The stories, for all their gentle appeal, are
not weak, or obtrusively effeminate. There is, in fact, what Margaret Lane calls a "seam of toughness" running just below Potter's dewy-fresh surfaces. The writer, unlike the more sublime
benign humorists, alludes slightly to such diverse themes as nature's deeper secrets, survival of the fittest, and the omnipres-
ent threat posed to her animal world constantly being menaced
by a human world which somehow believes that it is more important. But if Potter was obliquely aware of the twentieth-century
problems existing beyond her beloved Lake District, she never
lets threat or turmoil penetrate her slim but secure *oeuvre*.
Potter's stories are realistic glimpses for the young, while for
the "adult readers" the stories are imaginative renderings of
past memories when people and animals could remain timid without ever encountering exploitation and death. For the older readers who have read Potter's books when younger, the stories
remind them of an existence "touchingly [unlike] their own."[102]

The Adolescence of Bertie Wooster

In a curious but certain way, the literature of English humorist P. G. Wodehouse, which catalogs the "muckings" and misad-
ventures of the unparalled literary team of Bertie Wooster and
Jeeves, is an example of *a* "children's literature." If it cannot
be read by the very young, it still has an appeal to all readers

whose memories of childhood are significantly strong enough to make them feel that "maturity" is, in some regards, vastly overrated. The Wooster-Jeeves saga is a series of delightful stories which tell of the merry Knut Bertie Wooster's constant dalliances with friends who, like Wooster, are content to live life joyously. Indeed, Wodehouse's *oeuvre* has all the appeal of fixed adolescence.

The team of Wooster and Jeeves is fantastically synchronized, splendidly in tune; Wodehouse moves through England's countryside and in and out of the "metrop" (London) in numerous short stories and novels which never overstay their visit. Although he never matures or ages, and although he has the same presence of mind as a dolphin and offers little else than constant tootering, Bertie Wooster is one of English literature's most fascinating characters. But the characters of Wooster and his valet Jeeves have remained so elusive—while seeming so simple—that there has never been a critical consensus attending the literature of Wodeshouse's splendidly cocked tandem.

In all of English comic literature, there is no character more benignly innocent than Bertram Wilberforce Wooster. Where his valet, Jeeves (the real power behind the throne), is delightfully gothic—all eerie passages of melancholic detachment—Bertie Wooster is little more than an impressionistic puff of fun, sun, and light wind. Wodehouse creates ticklish but easy dilemmas for Wooster and Jeeves. Many solutions are available to the Knut; and after his rather hedonistic philosophy of life seems to go wrong, Bertie is constantly told by Jeeves to "read-up" on Nietzsche, Spinoza, and Hegel. For Wooster, of course, the names are just so much "spumoni" as he suspects there are better ways to turn the "absurdity" of the human condition into "mere looniness." Like the cushioned worlds of other benign humorists, Wodehouse's lands are extraterrestrial and age-tight. Consequently, Bertie Wooster and Jeeves continued in the 1970s (*Jeeves and the Tie That Binds,* 1971) in the same Georgwardian ways established in the collection of short stories *My Man Jeeves* (1917). Indeed, the team of Wooster and Jeeves has, over fifty-years time, been maintained in a hedonistic but benign world suspended in a timeless middle-earth untouched by the twentieth-century maladoption of sexuality, technology, and cultural fall-out and litter.

Like William S. Gilbert, Wodehouse is unabashedly fond of farcical methods, means by which he creates the delightfully confused characterizations which walk through the writer's labyrinthian and "odd-boddikin" plots. Wodehouse's plots, however, are little more than frames which he fills with print-outs of language programmed and spoiling for fun. Few critics have made attempts to figure out and categorize Wodehouse's language. But once again, as it is with the criticism of Milne, Carroll, and Edward Lear, critical analysis of Wodehouse's work is misdirected as it asks "What does this language say," when it should be asking "What is this language?" Even the kinder critics have been forced into loquacious nondefinitions when established criteria and literary theory fail. For Richard Voorhees, Wodehouse's language "is admirably clear, a mad and marvellous variegation." [140] Wodehouse has. according to Richard Usborne, "taught the English language to turn hand-springs for him, to lift weights, and to walk a tight-rope letting-off fireworks."[105] More confusing, however, is the criticism of R. B. D. French who sees Wodehouse's literature and language growing, not from literary inventiveness or the comic sensibility, but from what French calls "faithfulness to social manners and tastes which Wodehouse enjoys too much to abandon."[106] It seems rather beside the point (in a literary sense) to know that Wodehouse prefers a *demitasse* to a mug of stout, crystal to glass, pounds to pence, and the aristocracy to service. (In the same way, of course, it also matters little to know that Lewis Carroll might have been an infatuist who had something more than detached interest in little, yellow-haired girls when he wrote his Alice books; that Walter de la Mare wrote precious rhymes while checking statements in the Bank of England where he was secretary; that Beatrix Potter baked a mean blackbird pie; and that A. A. Milne wrote fussy failures which he brought to the London stage.)

The language of Wodehouse has a jungle-exotic quality as it tangles like vines around the plots which delightfully delay Bertie's maturity. Wodehouse takes the language of others, most notably Shakespeare, Thackeray, and Dickens, and ties it into his *own* slangy and gallantly archaic knots. Far from "cribbing" from these writers, Wodehouse uses their language for little more than eye-wash. And if some would dismiss his language and literature for being "too frisky, idiomatic, and colloquial," the problem is inherent in the assumption that literature is unworthy if it is frisky, idiomatic, and colloquial.

Where Lewis Carroll and, more often, Edward Lear, switch letters, words, and sentences around and into the curious obedience of disobedient order, Wodehouse invents a nonsense language that is defined as such by its realization from out of the mouth of Wooster. Carroll's nonsense is borne out of invention and rocked in airy cradles, while Wodehouse's language is developed from a reportage of Bertie's misadvantures in romantic homes, and especially from his discourses with friends in spas, *ristorantes,* and Droning clubs where he and his friends, too long on lunch, lift the beaker and bib and force rhetoric into "reespektuhbull" incoherence.

Always an indication of frequently iconic and nonsense language is the difficulty encountered when translating a comic language into another language. To translate Wodehouse's Bertie Wooster-Jeeves stories is to know what it means to be "bonkers." The French translators, although quite willing and able to turn "sardines" into "bacon," pad with a *jeux d'esprit;* and when Wooster utters "it reminded me of those lines in the poem 'see how the little, how does it go, tum, tumty, tiddly push?,'" the French translation is "Vois jouer les paurrets pom, pom, pom dix."[107] German translations, however, realize the antithesis of benign humor and as Wodehouse narrates:

> At the open window of the great library at Blandings Castle, drooping like a wet sock, as was his habit when he had nothing to prop his spine against, the Earl of Emsworth, that amiable and bone-headed peer, stood gazing, observing his domain. . . .[108]

the German translation is typically severe and economic: "Am offenen Verandofenster in Schoss stand Lord Emsworth und blikte auf siene weiten Damagen."[109]

Nonsense language pours from Bertie Wooster as all "intellectual umbrellas" seem "mere to the core," while "fat vegetables" and fruits are "served on maroon-cruises." On board ship, Bertie's nonsensical friends, much to Jeeve's dismay, show a penchant for throwing food and rubbing it into "wasted wallpapers." Wodehouse's inventive language, unlike Lewis Carroll's and to some extent Edward Lear's, does not depend so much on the singular and inner originality of words and phrases, but more on its bizarre placement in and subsequent issuance from such perpetually foreign places as the merry Knut's mouth. But Wodehouse "can flair a word" now and then, and what Bertie's cronies see as "tight spots," Bertie recognizes as "fricasses" and "probs," "deep into the mottled oyster." While others can't wait to say "goodbye" to him, Bertie exhibits the easy, if unrelaxed sophistication of the dilettante as he responds with a "pip-pip," a "teuf-teuf," and a "tinkerty-tonk."

Wodehouse's Bertie Wooster is, perhaps, the most "childish" element in twentieth-century children's literature. Bertie is a permanent juvenile and fake-flirt with the romantic dash and potency of an eleven-year-old boy. He is literature's fawn on the loose, doe-eyed, rubber-necked, and muddy-pawed. He is a record of deceived and disguised genes uttering their protest in a language of advanced baby-talk. Frequently, when Wooster hears himself speak, he becomes so excited by his own melodies that his emotions build and crest—a momentum similar to that motion and accumulating affection in Milne's Pooh stories when Christopher Robin pinks, flushes, and reddens into his "I love you." Bertie Wooster, speaking to his surrogate parent, Jeeves, in the novel *Very Good Jeeves,* says:

> "What-Ho, Jeeves," I said, entering the room where he waded knee-deep in suitcases and winter suitings like a sea-beast among the rocks. "Packing?" 'Yes, sir,' replied the honest fellow, for there are no secrets between us.
> "Pack on!" I said approvingly, "Pack, Jeeves, pack with care. Pack in the presence of the passenjare." And I rather fancy I added the words "tra-la" for I was in a merry mood.

Kenneth Grahame and Walter de la Mare create universes for their characters; Wodehouse creates a character in Jeeves who *is* the cosmos. Jeeves, in fact, is a literary force of which even Wodehouse seems to lose control. In fact, the writer has revealed that he never meant to continue the character of Jeeves at all (thirty-four short stories, ten novels) but, as he understates it, the character "just took hold and held on."[111] Jeeves is the magical midwife who directs the birth of looniness which sits on Wooster's blue lips and which swirls in his good heart. Jeeves is a benign force who insures the hunky-dory existence of Bertie as he allows the foppish knut to tipple out of leather flasks and stick his nose in jam jars. Like Walter de la Mare's sprites and fairies, who mysteriously issue in and out of his precious verses, Wodehouse's valet "manifests" and "shimmers" into the mahogany-heavy and leather-lined libraries in baronial homes which leave their doors open for him, and not, as Bertie thinks, for the gallant, run-amok. But where de la Mare's fairies are all butterflyed children and highly placed miniatures, Jeeves is the ethereal mystic who helps Bertie select an appropriate waistcoat, the correct muffler, the right cuff links. Even Jeeves is fallible in Wodehouse's benign saga, and no amount of stares, pinches, and pins can redress the sartorial disaster that is Bertie Wooster.

It is the character of Bertie Wooster, the sartorial, social, and intellectual adventurer, that gives Wodehouse's literature its definition as benign humor. Bertie's situation is always comic, for the English Ozzie Nelson is never on-the-job, constantly befuddled but ready for ice cream. Life is all strawberries for Wooster despite everyone's absolute realization that he will always be "knee-deep" in the eternal "bisque of things." Bertie, however, is an artful dodger who gobbles his "toothsome" eggs and spreads his marmalade on the melba while donning the tweeds on his way to another plotted and linguistic misadventure.

In some ways, Bertie Wooster is the most benign force in children's literature. He hates no one, he is chivalrous, gallant, and ignorant of the techniques of hurtful gossip and spiteful revenge—all this while he listens to assorted aunts call him

"an excrescence" a "blot on the globe," Bertie, no masochist,
loves them all.

In the final analysis, definers of "children's literature" must
consider, not only the appeal and possibility of a literature which
certain, specific age groups understand and enjoy, but the realization that children's literature, (even if one accepts that it is
written for "younger" people) has linguistic and even extra-
linguistic attractions for "older" readers who want to remember
and forget.

5.
Benign Humor: Fabulous and Fantastic

The works of Kenneth Grahame and Walter de la Mare range from the fabulous to the fantastic. Walter de la Mare is benign humor's historian and choreographer of fairylands, while Kenneth Grahame, the fantasist and "beast-fabulist" created the masterpiece of benign literature, *The Wind in the Willows.* Grahame's story is stocked by fabulous beasts who live in a netherland created by Grahame, benevolent and ordered and grown in a language that is lyrical and sensuous.

Kenneth Grahame's The Wind in the Willows

Kenneth Grahame's animals are fabulously human and quite recognizable even though the writer builds legends about them— legends to which Grahame gives mythic dimension. *The Wind in the Willows,* with its mythic and fabulous dimensions, has the quality of folded dreams which Grahame wanted to remember. His masterpiece is Grahame's search for what is lost in a modern time as the writer hedges and guards against lost opportunity and discovered decadence.

Always a fair indication of the artistry implicit in the works of the benign humorists is the confusion which greets their work. For Peter Green in *Kenneth Grahame: A Biography, The Wind in the Willows* is a "fantasy [by] which country gentlemen . . .

triumph over the unprincipled radical *canaille.*" Green sees
Grahame as the "fearful" countryman whose "loyalty . . . to
caste produced a book which hoped to preserve a pre-industrial
society. . . ." Green concludes that not only is the book violent,
psychological, and even allegorical, but "mythic and mean" as
well.[112] Despite Green's attempt, the less pedantic critiques of
benign humor have always been the most satisfactory. In her
survey of children's literature, May Hill Arbuthnot rightly sub-
stitutes feeling for pedantic analyses. Arbuthnot is struck by the
continual kindness of literary animals to one another and the ways
in which Grahame endows his story with a sense of safety and
"sanctuary." The book is populated, she continues, with "understanding hearts" and "overlooked mistakes." For Arbuthnot,
The Wind in the Willows is "gemmed."[113]

Grahame's apogeic story tells of the adventures of four
animals — Toad, the Water Rat, Mole, and Badger. And while
among nature's less attractive creations, the four are given human characteristics which seem to wear better on "fur-people."
Toad is the central character. He is brusque, vain, and boister-
ous as he indulges his weakness for stealing automobiles — cars
he drives with admirable abandon into walls and onto front
lawns. Essentially, *The Wind in the Willows* is the adventure
of Toad after he steals a jitney, "cracks it" and is sentenced to
jail. Toad escapes and, with Homeric determination, he finds his
way, like Ulysses, across incident-filled lands bringing him
back to "Toad Hall," his home which earlier had been taken
over by such assorted nondescripts as ferrets, weasels, and an
occasional squirrel. With the help of Rat, Mole, and Badger,
Toad drives them from Toad Hill with a swaggering display of
military acumen and bluff bravado. After his victory, Toad meta-
morphoses into a temporarily modest and chastened frog.

Grahame's story offers certain heuristic pleasures as various themes emerge including the despoiling of the environment
by man, a yearning for a "golden past" and halcyon delights,
and the efficacy of remaining loyal to a rigid class system. The
story, on a less successful level, can also be read as Homeric
myth. But more significantly, *The Wind in the Willows* offers
sensuous and tactile pleasures which all but obfuscate the arid-

ity of common, catholic themes. Grahame's book is best apprehended through the reader's indulgence of sounds, sights, and
smells. *Willows* is replete with "crackling-fresh" grass and
"dewy-sweet" gardens. In addition, the book is fragrant with
food. Smell is everywhere as "... she carried a tray with a
cup of fragrant tea steaming on it; and a plate piled-up with very
hot, buttered toast, cut thick, very brown on both sides, with the
butter running through the holes in it in great golden
drops...."[114] Grahame fills the air with such rich language
that the reader feels tempted to chew on its sound, encouraged
to feel the smells.

The book details a "hummocky," pastoral land spread in
"purple loose-strife where the willow herb is... tender and
wistful," and "where pink clouds and sunsets" go hand in hand
with "amber jerkins," "shepherd boys," and "nymphs." Grahame turns description into drug, and the appropriately aban-
doned reader becomes dizzy and delightfully lost in such bitter-
sweet passages as

> stores ... are visible everywhere ... piles of apples, turnips,
> and potatoes, baskets full of nuts and jars of honey; but the
> two little white beds on the remainder of the floor looked
> soft and inviting and the linen on them, though coarse was
> clean and smelt beautifully of lavender, and the Mole and
> the Water Rat, shaking off their garments in some thirty
> seconds, tumbled in between the sheets in great joy and
> contentment.[115]

Grahame's "Wild Wood," like de la Mare's "faeryland" is
drawn in miniature. As a result, Grahame's brooding woods lack
threat and terror. The animals' homes are small and dear, set
in river holes and in sides of snow banks where solid doors with
"iron bell-pulls" hang next to "small brass plates" on which
the proud beasts engrave their initials.[116]

Unlike those benign humorists who tend to overuse literary device, Grahame seems almost inadvertently to have gotten humor
from the emotion and flow of a sudden discovery of descriptive
prose. Frequently, the humor comes as epiphany, much like the
Mole, standing in the road with "... his heart torn asunder,
and a big sob gathering... [leaping] up ... in passionate

escape."[117] *The Wind in the Willows* is, at the same time,
ecstatic and melancholy, mystical and real, sweet and aching,
innocent but knowing. Such contradictions make the book difficult to get at. There is, for example, something ineffable and
voiceless in such passages as

> The Water Rat was restless, and he did not know exactly
> why, to all appearances the summer's pomp was still at
> fullest height and although in the tilled acres, green had
> given way to gold, though rowans were reddening and the
> woods were dashed here and there with a tawny fierceness,
> yet light and warmth and color were still present. . . .[118]

The language of *Willows* balances between mystery and solution as the reader wonders about worlds of "wheat, yellow, wavy
and murmurous..."[119] and the sounds of "...phantom
song[s] pealing high between vaporous grey, wave-lapped
walls."[120] There is something quite melancholy about the
strange and peripatetic bird which comes to the wood and tells
Rat, "Why, sometimes I dream of the shell-fish of Marseilles,
and I wake up crying."[121] Grahame's Toad, Water Rat, Mole,
and Badger, like A. A. Milne's Pooh, Tigger, Owl, and Eeyore,
are animals with hearts that flutter in ecstasy. The Rat, for example, knows the enchantments of small apprehensions as he
looks into the river and exclaims "O! the blessed coolness!"[122]
For Grahame, locked secrets and the unknowable are factors of
benign humor. Consequently, in the chapter, "The Piper at the
Gates of Dawn," Grahame sounds the religiously appropriate
response as Rat and Mole shudder as they encounter what must
surely be a God. The animals, very much in awe, whisper to each
other

> "Rat," he found breath to whisper, shaking, "Are you
> afraid?"
> "Afraid?" murmured the Rat, his eyes shining with un-
> utterable love. "Afraid! of Him? O, never, never!
> And yet-and yet-O Mole, I am afraid!"[123]

Kenneth Grahame enjoyed a curious and perverse literary advantage similar to that enjoyed by the American poet Wallace

Stevens. Just as Stevens could cultivate "Blue Guitars" in a poetic sensibility while checking the flow of premiums into an in-
surance company of which he was a vice-president, Grahame
indulged his imagination while Secretary of the Bank of England. While some friends asked him why he wanted to "get
mixed-up with beauty," Grahame spent hours in banking—time
spent, apparently, in viewing the intrinsic "absurdity" and humor in the human species. Although he saw human existence as
absurd and troubled, Grahame would not offer socio-literary
antidotes. Grahame felt that to offer commentary and criticism
on social and cultural problems through his literature would be
to dilute the purity of the alternative existence he built in *The
Wind in the Willows.* Grahame knew, as did all the benign
humorists, that the wits and satirists would take care of
trouble. The writer was pained, however, when he saw man ruin-
ing the environment and, in *The Wind in the Willows,* he gently
but surely scores those who leave "brambles and tree roots
behind them, confusedly heaped and tangled."[124] He saw
woods being leveled, but he opted for the literary, nonresist-
ance of benign humor.

Grahame, even though a consummate fantasist, was first the
benign humorist. As a result, he let vague and only slightly disruptive realities intrude on his miniature dreamworld as he
realized that total fantasy, coupled with the intoxicating nature
of his descriptive prose, could result in a work which would
seem inordinately exaggerated, even surreal. Therefore, Grahame's beasts suffer cuts and bruises and fall prey to brittle
egos and the faults of personality. There is much fight between
and among Toad, Mole, Rat, and Badger, but they always realize that fighting will help them love each other better.

Grahame, both in a literary and personal sense, was sparing
in his criticism of England's rigid class structure which, by
the Edwardian years, was trying to mend itself. In *The Wind in
the Willows,* there is a class system based on social present-
ability, amount of rhetoric, and leadership capabilities. Badger
is upper-upper class, Toad is upper class, while Rat and Mole
occupy a middle latitude. Ferrets and weasels, of course, are

very *de classe!* Each animal sees the one above as the ultimate authority and, significantly, are glad of it. Grahame
yearned for the time when harmony was possible in master-
servant relationships; and everyone works well when the ". . .
good natured Mole, having cut some slices of ham, set the
hedge-hogs to fry it, and returned to his own breakfast. , . ."[125]
It is wrong to conclude, however, that Grahame deals harshly,
even satirically, with class structure in such sentences as, "He
gave them sixpence apiece and a pat on the head and they went
with much respectful swinging of caps and touching of fore-
locks."[126] The writer's beastly class structure in *The
Wind in the Willows* is not based on a disdain of the upper
class, or on a championing of the downtrodden. Instead, Badger,
Toad, Rat, Mole, et al., are put into class structures according
to wisdom, talent, and resourcefulness rather than through
length of bloodlines and extent of banking accounts. Within their
class and according to the respective functions of service, all
the animals in *The Wind in the Willows* have beyond-life-time
security and Badger remarks "Who can tell. . . . People come
and they stay for awhile, they flourish, they build—and they go.
It is their way. But, we remain. . . . We are an enduring lot.
. . . And so it will ever be."[127]

   Indeed, Kenneth Grahame's animals have a special place in
English literature. Toad could tell the more severe critics of
light literature that if they "could grow tails and sport fur,"
then they would understand

>   And then they heard the angels tell,
>   'Who were the first to cry Nowell?'
>   Animals all, as it befell,
>   In the stable where they did dwell!
>   Joy shall be their's in the morning![128]

The Inner Visions of Walter de la Mare

Literary "faery-lands" are so immaculately rendered in Walter de la Mare's rhymes and verses that the writer is accurately called their chief architect and historian. De la Mare's stories, verses, and rhymes, however, are much more than fey and brittle pieces of literature. For the "young" reader, they are voyages in bathtubs which hold the water of the world; for the "older" reader they are "other-worldish" and ". . . above or beyond topicality."[129]

De la Mare's miniature worlds were created by a writer who remained more hopeful about existence than even some of the benign humorists. His sonorous songs, verses, and simple rhymes are filled with shadows that delight. De la Mare denies the "inherent morbidity" of even death as he is curiously fascinated by its "impassioned beauty." De la Mare obliquely uses the theme of death to *materialize* the "faery-lands" of his verses and rhymes. He believes in ghosts and spectres, and in his literature he humorizes them. In de la Mare's works, death is but a harbinger for another born spirit—brought to populate a slowly diminishing "faery-world."

De la Mare's *Songs for Childhood* represent his most artful contribution to benign humor. The ethereal songs seem afloat in angel hair as the writer offers verses that are magic, easy, precise, and fair. Indeed, *Songs for Childhood* are most enjoyed by young readers who recognize the unarguably fantastic—young minds that realize the unattractive futility of return trips back to where unreality isn't. For the young reader, *Songs for Childhood* offer a shiver unqualified in time and experience. De la Mare's rhymes and verses reduce cosmologies into fluttering fairy wings and piling tinker toys. The reduction does not diminish understanding, and as Doris Ross McCrosson points out, de la Mare was Blakean enough to know that a child could see the world in a grain of sand and eternity in an hour.[130]

De la Mare was a utopian writer who seemed to know almost instinctively that there is a "pre-Edenic peace" in a world written and weighed on small scales and in small hearts.[131] Too

often critics have continued to look for *big* literary things in
de la Mare's literature, and when they find none they make
small conclusions. A good example of critical zeal is Doris
McCrosson's conclusion about de la Mare's concept of the
"impossible she." McCrosson comes critically acropper, however, with her thesis that much of de la Mare's work fits "perfectly" into Jung's concept of the "anima."[132] A tentative
approach to the literature of de la Mare is always the surest
way to get a sense of the poetry. Surer than McCrosson's theory
is the criticism of Forest Reid. Reid writes de la Mare's
"poetry of imagination and vision with its hints of loneliness
[belongs] to a world perhaps remembered, perhaps only dreamed
about but which, at least is not this world."[133]

A critical and territorial empathy is important to an understanding of the artistry of the benign humorists. And where the
descriptive felicities of Milne and the brooding beauty of Potter
indicate a certain distance between the writers and their halcyon literary worlds, de la Mare's writings seem to report on
places in which he actually lived. With his verses and rhymes,
de la Mare relives "the gold of his childhood." He believes that
"in the lonely dreams of a child there [is] a grace, a clarity,
which is dulled to extinction by the growth of worldly wisdom."
In fact, for de la Mare, "adulthood" means the necessity to escape back to the hauntings of his childhood.[134]

De la Mare crafted his books in the "ether" of modern time,
but the writer was so disenchanted with the nervous but spiritu-
ally and morally anaesthetic new century that he wrote verses
he hoped to materialize in such a way that he could use them as
a literal, if literary escape back to what he referred to as the
"golden glow" of his "dreams of sleep." In his "dreams of
sleep," de la Mare's witchery is complete as every sandbox becomes a sanctuary, every shovel a magic wand. De la Mare's
stories and verses describe sweet, alternative lands that are
milked and honeyed and populated by enchantments both "uffish"
and elfish. It is apparent that the English countryside, so often a
staple of the artistic expressions of poets, painters and writers,
was not beautiful enough for Walter de la Mare.

If de la Mare's stories and verse seem edged in mystery and mysticism, they are first ". . . humor which assuages the tension and actually enhances the unabashed beauty of the telling."[135] The writer's humor is fraught with fantasy, but it remains unforced and unpredictable as it issues from purple bushes, cameo clouds, wildflowers, skunk cabbages, and floating seeds growing in just above-ground soil farmed by a vaporous and almost indolent magic. As a result, de la Mare's precious verses have been called "dusty," "rare," "quaint," and "filigree." To Harry Duffin, de la Mare's work is the quintessence of what the critic calls "beauty-humor." Duffin writes, "thus beautified, humor becomes a true facet of the dellamarian genius. It is a factor in divine life and vision." Duffin adds "If there is a laughter in heaven it will not be that kind of laughter, which Hobbes defined as 'a passion of sudden glory,' but a passion of delight in some surprising display of beauty and love."[136]

With de la Mare's literature, as with the less ornate stories of A. A. Milne and Beatrix Potter, the reader must not conclude that what seems to be children's literature is, somehow, less literate and, consequently, less worthy of a mature consideration. At times it seems as though de la Mare didn't write for children at all. Duffin writes:

> He illuminates childhood, he is illuminated by the echoing memories of its eternal hours. Childhood is a crystal, and he who can hold it in his hand, shall see deep into the heart of things, and may hope to die as he lived—a child. The mature mind should still be a garden; but there is an Eden of the heart, a fellowship with innocence that only children know.[137]

In the 1902 collection of verse and rhymes entitled *Songs of Childhood*, de la Mare feeds on an adult mystery as he draws on his special gift to make the implausible believable as spirits and wood nymphs come glowing out of the dewy-days to tickle the lips of robins and jays. In these sublime songs, hushes and whispers and smiles are caught by "faeries" who nourish on small food-stuffs and who catch butterflies and bees in order to hand-feed them petals and honey.

Despite the designed simplicity of *Songs of Childhood,* de la Mare uses a parochial but highly effective device to create a wandering and unpredictable humor. He obtains a nervous and slight humor from the apparently unassuming and unamusing vanities his people use to demystify their lives. In "Lovelocks," a vain and ethereal Lady Caroline settles in front of her mirror where she takes hours to fix her hair into complex ringlets and convoluted coils before going out to visit. But outside her windows, the weather is unremittingly cruel. Inexplicably, the trance of her vanity continues as Lady Caroline passes her hands, "white in the candleshine," across and "twixt the coils."[138]

Even when taking a turn towards nonsensical rhyme and verse de la Mare's benign humor is replete with simple but splendid imagery; in the poem "Tartary," mystery-fish swim and "slant" in pools, "their fins athwart the sun."[139] While there is a certain imagistic fierceness in "Tartary," there are definitive, if uneasy smiles as well. In the third stanza there is an enigmatic but swash-buckling humor:

> If I were Lord of Tartary,
>   I'd wear a robe of beads,
> White and gold, and green they'd be—
>   And small and thick as seeds;
> And ere should wane the morning star,
> I'd don my robe and scimitar,
> And zebras seven should draw my car
>   Through Tartary's dark glades.[140]

In the stanza, de la Mare stalks masculine threat, but the hunt has all the terror of a halloween spook.

De la Mare is purposely artless but certainly delightful when he gleans too easily obtained humor through the mere motions of his versification. But unlike the meaningless and thus delightful nonsense of Edward Lear's rhymes and limericks, de la Mare draws sense from sound. In "Down-adown-derry" there is modest and gracious humor in the flow of lines in the first stanza.

Down-adown-derry,
Sweet Annie Maroon,
Gathering daisies
In the meadowes of Doone,
Sees a white fairy
Skip buxom and free
Where the waters go brawling
In rills to the sea;
   Singing down-adown-derry.[141]

The writer of beauty-humor is less frequently but more deliberately nonsensical than Lewis Carroll. De la Mare, for example, makes use of an "ironical nonsense" in the verse which finds "a sailor in the wood"—a wood where "every shrill and long-drawn note, like bubbles breaks in me."

The incongruent imagery so much a staple of benign humor since its development in Lewis Carroll's *Alice* stories is resplendent in de la Mare's verses. In addition to a visual incongruence, there is sound incongruity in the precious images in de la Mare's "The Huntsman."

Three jolly gentlemen,
   In coats of red,
Rode their horses
   Up to bed.

Three jolly gentlemen
   Snored till morn,
Their horses champing
The golden corn.

Three jolly gentlemen
   At break of day,
Came clitter-clatter down the stairs
And galloped away.[142]

De la Mare's use of nonsense language, however, is contrived and exotic, hence less satisfying *in terms* of benign humor than the more grounded nonsense of Carroll. But there is nothing artless and uninteresting about de la Mare's part semitic, part Swahili, and part gentlemanly use of language in the stanza:

Talaheeti sul magloon
Olgar, ulgar Manga-moon;
Ah-mi Sulani!
Tishnar sootli maltmahee
Ganganareez soongalee.
Manni Mulgar sang suwhee:
Sulani, ghar magleer.[143]

In the late nineteenth and early twentieth centuries, the influence of Lewis Carroll's "Jabberwocky" was preeminent in the nonsensical efforts of benign humorists. In de la Mare's "Andy's Battle Song" there is the post-jabberwocky of

Voice without a body,
Panther of black Roses,
Jack-alls fat on icicles,
Ephelanto, Aligatha,
Zevvara and Jaccatray,
Unicorn and River-horse;
    Ho, ho, ho!
Here's Andy Battle,
Waiting for the enemy!

Imbe Calandola,
M'Keesso and Quesanga,
Dondo, Sharamomba
Pongo and Enjekko,
Millions of Monkeys,
Rattlesnake and scorpion,
Swamp and death and shadow,
    Ho, ho, ho!
Come on, all of ye,
Here's Andy Battle,
Waiting and-alone![144]

But where the sensuous nonsense of Carroll, and, to a lesser degree Kenneth Grahame, is highly linguistic, de la Mare's nonsense verse is more visually derivative, more dependent on sensory incongruity. His verses have the sheer uplift of descriptive nonsense, and in "Bandog" someone asks,

Has anyone seen my Mopser?—
    A comely dog is he,
With hair of the colour of a Charles the Fifth,
    And teeth like ships at sea,

His tail it curls straight upwards,
   His ears stand two abreast,
And he answers to the simple name of Mopser,
   When civilly addressed.[145]

It is more than rhetorically fanciful to conclude that de la
Mare's verses and rhymes are more Winnie the Poe than Winnie the Pooh. The verses are simple yet fierce, plain but gothic.
The artistry of de la Mare is again implicit in the realization
that, like Lewis Carroll and Kenneth Grahame, he gives humorous expression to words that seem, when isolated from context,
quite lacking in humor. In the third stanza of "Captain Lean,"
there is inexplicable humor in

Powder was violets to his nostrils,
   Sweet the din of the fighting-line,
Now he is flotsam on the seas,
And his bones are bleached with brine.[146]

In *Songs of Childhood,* "huggers" and "muggers" ghost about
"gallipots" and "grottos." De la Mare knew that white sheets
with eye and nose holes cut into them were surefire amuse-
ments. The writer also knew juvenile hearts, and he knew the
quickening interest in, and the implicit humor of, the masquerade.
In "Apple Charm", a poem appearing in *Poems for Children*
(1930), he writes:

I plucked an apple, sleek and red,
I took his three black pips,
Stuck two upon my cheek, and brow
   And t'other on my lips

Dick on my cheek, the other Tom
But O-my love to be—
Robin that couched upon my lip
   Was truest unto me.[147]

With "The Apple Charm," de la Mare *hints* at something post-
pubescent—a thought he will not allow to linger lest the reader
be inappropriately distracted by it. (In the same regard, one
wishes Leslie Fiedler hasn't been so touched by Nigger Jim's
call to "Huck honey.") De la Mare, however, was not untouched

by considerations extrinsic to his poetic faery-worlds, and in
Crossings: A Fairy Play (1921) the political note is soft but
audible in:

> There sate Good Queen Bess, oh,
> A-shining on her throne.
> Up Jessie; down, docket;
> *My money's gone!*[148]

De la Mare was a master at developing humor out of life's inevitable but small puzzles. In "The Tulip" (*Stuff and Nonsense,
and So On* [1927]) there is humor-in-dotage, smiles in senes-
cence, as de la Mare offers solutions in

> There was an old Begum of Frome,
> There was an old Yogi of Leicester;
> She sent him a tulip in bloom,
> He rolled his black eyes and he blessed her.
>
> How replete with delight
> Is a flower to the sight!
> It brightens the day and it sweetens the night.
> Oh! if all the old ladies grew tulips in Frome,
> How happy the yogis of Leicester![149]

Similar to Milne in the "Pooh" stories, de la Mare, likes to
state a problem which he can resolve simply, syllogistically. In
"The Duet;"

> There was a young lady of Tring,
> There was an olde Fellow of Kello.
> And she-she did nothing but sing,
> And he-he did nothing but bellow:
>
> Now I think (and don't you?),
> that the best thing to do
> Were to marry these two;
> Then maybe the one would sing no more in Tring,
> Or the other not bellow in Kello.[150]

Inside de la Mare's faery-world "real" things are golden
clouds, purple catches of wings, sapphire swirls and lavender
hills. His verses have the buzz of mystery and the speed of un-
recorded history. But de la Mare is always careful not to dis-
turb the inescapable tranquillity of an alien world above the

fray. In the verse "Puss" (*Poems for Children* [1930]), the
reader is warned but warmed.

> Puss loves man's winter fire
> Now that the sun so soon
> Leaves the hours cold it warmed
> In burning June.
>
> She purrs full length before
> the heaped-up hissing blaze,
> Drowsy in slumber-down
> Her head she lays.
>
> While he with whom she dwells
> Sits snug in his inglenook,
> stretches his legs to the flames
> And reads his book.[151]

De la Mare's less enigmatic verses build a euphoria out of
abandonment. And there is the humor of ecstasy in these gust-
ing and gay verses:

> Fol, dol, do, and a south wind a-blowing O,
> Fol, dol, do, and green growths a-growing O,
> Fol, dol, do, and the heart inside me knowing O,
>   Tis merry, merry month of May.
>
> Fol, dol, do, shrill chanticleers a-crowing O,
> Fol, dol, do, and the mowers soon a-mowing O,
> O lovelier than the lilac tree, my lovely loves a-showing O,
>   In merry, merry month of May.[152]

The writer was especially fond of out-of-hand verses and rhymes
exhibiting the humor implicit in brevity and the dialectical humor
resulting from amusing manipulation of sound. "Sam Lover,"
for example, ends before it seems to begin as "Poor Sam Lover,
Now turf do cover; His wildness over."[153] It seems to matter little in a literary sense that there is something inane about
"The Mouse," where

> In a snug little house,
> Which I shared with my Fanny,
> Lives a mite of a mouse,
> And we called it Magnani.[154]

De la Mare, like most of the more accomplished benign humorists, is fond of coined language. He exercises this literary largesse in such mapped-words as momotumbo, manaqua, desdado, tim-tam, yookoo, clutemnacious, chalatenanaga. Many of de la Mare's critics, however, conditioned to look with disdain at alternative languages, see a *Mexicali-Esperanto* predilection in the writer's coined words as they confuse "chilly" with "chili."

De la Mare, like his fellow humorists, never asked critics and readers to suck at his lines, to pocket the eggs. He only cautioned them not to forget what has become a literary truism for the writer of benign humor: that "there is nothing to me but more than what you seemingly think you can't see."

Kenneth Grahame and Walter de la Mare created "extraterritorial" lands out of traditional languages untraditionally used and from literary devices that never seem mannered. Both Grahame and de la Mare believed in the benevolence of order; if *The Wind in the Willows* and de la Mare's songs and verses seem expressions of unreal places and behaviors, it is simply the writers' way to offer an alternative to the disorder of their times.

That pessimism does not intrude on their literature is not the least of their literary achievements.

6.
The Language of Benign Humor

The language of the benign humorists remains isolated from traditional forms and free of whimsical scholarship. Criticism, for example, has not dealt well or fairly with the language and literature of such humorists as P. G. Wodehouse and A. A. Milne. Even contemporary critics and literary scholars remain misled by a language that seems all laze, impressionistic puffs, and cellophane-uplifts since, by the twentieth century, any literature daring to deal exclusively in smiles and fun was considered inappropriate for times which had turned grave and severe.

But the more accomplished benign humorists steadied and continued to use a language that ran counter to the times. Their extra literary skin, however, was not so thick that they could deny feeling the pinch of the new century. But social concerns remained inside as they wrote a literature-on-the-mend with a language before unseen.

While the language of the nineteenth-century wits exhibited the stylized dash of overheated thoughts and distempered visions, the literature of the benign humorists seems cool, simple, and foam-born as it continues to give linguistic path to the *litterateurs* of childhood, the fabulist and the fantasist. So while the literary and journalistic wits swaggered past the fin de siecle bearding many literary critics with rhetorical punch and flourish, the humorists drew on "timeless inner-languages." Their new languages were not, however, an indication that the humorists of benign literature knew little about traditional languages. Instead, new languages grew from their dismissal of traditional languages as the humorists suspected that the late nineteenth and twentieth centuries wanted more. The benign humorists cannot be faulted for those who would confuse blithe spirits with gullibility, and "alternative language" with "primitive thinking." It is not surprising that this new and aberrative language outstrips such finely tuned and theoretical minds as that of Benjamin Whorf.

Whorf, like other linguists, semanticists, and lexicographers, feels that a word—an *isolato*—is "without meaning" when not afforded the contextual benefit of sentence. If considered *within* the context of traditional languages, Whorf is inescapably correct. It seems equally apparent, however, that contextual ratification is not always necessary when determining the sense of individual words within the language of benign humor. In A. A. Milne's sentence, "It is a haycorn," for example, the *meaning* of the word "haycorn" is all in the word itself—alive in its iconic shell; to know what "It," "is" and "a" mean does little to interpret the individual meaning of "haycorn." First and unqualified impressions about the language of the benign humorists are not the worst ways by which to *intuit* its meaning. For example, "haycorn" might mean a form of "acorn," or it could mean something akin to a "hayfield." But what "haycorn" really is, is an "h," an "a," a "y," a "c," an "o," an "r," and an "n."

The language of the benign humorists is manifest in strings of "small" words and innocent ideas that seem more like beads and bubbles than sentences and theory. Many readers of the benign humorists have difficulty in understanding the language of the humorists when applying ordinary and established literary logic. Fortunately there are readers and critics who remain delightfully undaunted by even the nonsense language of Lewis Carroll. Marshall McLuhan, one of the more accomplished humorists of the 1960s, and anxious to pillage "the global village," (the place where "impressive words and thoughts betray us") is assured that Lewis Carroll's *non-use* of time in the Alice stories is an "infinitely better way to mark time." It is, theorizes McLuhan, a "kind of space time . . . which had its own space and its own time."[155] Surely, Lewis Carroll would have cared for that.

Adding a lot of a little to an understanding of the language of the benign humorists has been the work in the philosophy of language done by William P. Alston. Alston seems to understand better than most that certain language must be read, listened to, and "mulled-over," "reverberated into the air," and studied in the eyes before it can acquiesce into categories based on traditional constructs of language. If Alston is more guarded when he writes that "words must stand the test of empirical evaluation," he comes closer to an understanding of the language of the benign humorists when he theorizes that "it is an extremely important fact about language that it is possible to use a word intelligibly without using it in any of its senses."[156] Indeed, that is one of the reasons why Carroll's "green thoughts" continue to sleep "furiously."

An approach to the language of the benign humorist undertaken from "without" presumes the sacrosanct nature of applied linguistic theories which "grew up" in the nineteenth and twentieth centuries and had been weaned on the comic tradition implicit in the works of such "serious" humorists as Shakespeare, Congreve, Goldsmith, et al. Such theory is weaned on metaphor as it pays obsequious homage to "tradition for tradition's sake." Many such theories seem written in stone. Consequently, they discourage imaginative alternatives. Such imagination, however, is not absent in the criticism of a few academic scholars. For example, it has been suggested by one professor of English literature at a Boston university that criticism which denies "extra-literary contrivances" is "invalid." For her, admittedly intoxicated by light English literature, the respective *oeuvres* of such writers as Milne and Wodehouse are most enjoyably read and understood if undertaken in "a big, leather chair and fronted by a fire." She further indicates that it is helpful to drink during the reading—but only port or sherry, of course. She contends that such "controlled reading environments" help her to dodge critical predilections which threaten to "jack-hammer" into the stories.

I. A. Richards supports inventive language, writing it is "through the interaction of words *within* a language that a writer works."[157] In this regard, critics are to be encouraged to cultivate an empathy for the literature of Carroll to best *understand* the Alice stories, to be unbiased when assessing Milne's Pooh-books and P. G. Wodehouse's Bertie Wooster-Jeeves novels and short stories. It is unproductive to compare the literature of the benign humorists to other writers in the English, comic tradition. Indeed, such humorists as Milne, Potter, de la Mare, Grahame, and Wodehouse make the question of literary "association" academic. For these humorists, the truism which attends their art can be stated as follows: *what the language means is that it doesn't mean what it seems to mean since it is not conceived to mean at all.*

W. K. Wimsatt in his book, *The Verbal Icon,* suggests that coined words, such as Lewis Carroll's "brillig," are more appropriately literary than a "wrongly used correct word." Indeed, the language of the humorists is daring and audacious since the "iconicity" of *an* "extraterritorial" language "calls attention [only] to itself . . . and invites evaluation."[158] Such evaluation, undertaken from outside the traditional boundaries of criticism and within the guidelines, unstated but suggested by the humorists, bespeaks the need to develop critical criteria that encourage a new "critical relativism" and "sliding-scale" of criticism where literature is assessed on its own ground. It is wrong, for example, to conclude that the language and the literature of the benign humorists, like that of the early twentieth-century Dadaists is not *analyzable.* As Louis MacNiece neatly puts it, to analyze obscurity is like attempting "to open a box with a hidden lock. . . ." After the box is opened, of course, there is "nothing" inside but the "hidden-lock."[159] Herein, however, is an essential point which must not be overlooked. For once the box is open, *the "nothing" that is found inside is precisely what is found inside.* Many readers of the literature remain "unalerted" to the language of the humorists since it seems nothing more than an impossible vamp with "simplistic rhetoric," no matter how good a "read" it offers to those twentieth-century readers, perplexed and puzzled by their culture—those who saw art, by mid-century, turn into dated *moha* and optical pottage. Responsible critics must learn to slip their theory in between the pistachio patter of off-the-chocolate cuffs of the humorists' outrageous humans and endearing animals.

Perhaps, then, the readers and critics who judge Wodehouse's "mottled-oyster" bad metaphor will see it as a place for pearls.

Benign Language of Bertie Wooster and Pooh

The overwhelming quality of P. G. Wodehouse's language is its "coziness." It looks good, it feels right. It is familiar and comfortable. Unfortunately, many critics confuse "comfortable" and "familiar" with "careless" and "incestuous." But empathetic critics of Wodehouse learn to root in the leather and "pour with the tea." Such empathy to the language indicates that a literature which is unconcerned with societal puzzle and pedantic message is not necessarily unconcerned with the techniques of enjoyable art. To enjoy, and not worry over the literature, is more important than the considerations of pedantry.

The language of Wodehouse's Wooster-Jeeves sage, like that of Milne's Pooh books, Carroll's Alice stories, and de la Mare's "Songs of Childhood" does not breed in literary theory or methodology as it encourages the reader to get its feel, find its texture, test its flex. The sense of feel and texture is a subtle matter presuming that the discriminating reader at least wants to know how the language blows into baronial homes, harks into Wooster's clubs, drifts out of Lewis Carroll's snarking clouds, and burrows into Grahame's unearthy river-banks and Milne's tree-trunks. Certainly, the literature of the benign humorists is better tasted than swallowed. The reader who decides to analyze the language and literature of Wodehouse, for example, should expect to get caught up the silly and primrose path of Bertie Wooster's tongue, as the misspent knut speaks like a butterfly caught in brandy. Wodehouse's language typographically transcends the spilled Woosterese, as the words of the writer speed in hot sentences that seem tangled as they

reach the right margin in galloping, rhetorical muscles but turn
"toney" and sleek at the beginning of a new paragraph. The mus-
cle and speed of the language is supplied by Bertie and it is left
to Jeeves to tidy it up. Jeeves is asked by a concerned Wooster:

> "What did they quarrel about?"
> "They did not quarrel, sir. When his Lordship began to
> pay his addresses, the young person naturally flattered, be-
> gan to waver between love and ambition. But even now she
> has not formally rescinded the understanding."
> "Then if your scheme works and Uncle George edges out
> it will do your pal a bit of good?"
> "Yes, sir, Smethurst—his name is Smethurst—would con-
> sider it a consummation devoutly to be wished."
> "Rather well put that, Jeeves, Your own?"
> "No, sir, the Swan of Avon, sir."[160]

The only thing that "looms" in the stories of Bertie Wooster
and "his man Jeeves" is Wooster's herringbones and tweeds;
and the only thing that seems submerged in the saga, are the
pins and fasteners Jeeves uses to right Wooster's sartorial in-
accuracies. Wodehouse's language, however, is more than
missed stitches. Unlike Lewis Carroll's benign but somehow
foreboding Alice stories, unlike the excesses of ecstasy which
hit Pooh and Christopher Robin at hearts almost too achingly
pure and simple, unlike the faery lands of de la Mare which
threaten to recede as the reader puts on age, and unlike the animals of Kenneth Grahame threatened but untouched by English
"sportsmen" who hung cousin-quails in rashers of one hundred
on Edwardian lawns, Wodehouse's language feasts on the con-
stancies of total ignorance and benign bliss as Jeeves supplies
the laconic, "young master" with mufflers against embarrass-
ment, cold, and threat. The moments in the Wooster-Jeeves
saga of stories which seem fraught and tentative are the occasionally sharp exchanges between Bertie and Jeeves. In *The
Code of the Woosters,* for example, Jeeves suggests to the sar-
torially inept Bertie that "the trousers, perhaps a quarter of an
inch higher, sir. One aims at the carelessly graceful break over
the instep. It is a matter of the nicest adjustment." Bertie dis-
agrees and answers, "There are moments, Jeeves, when one

asks oneself, 'do trousers matter?' " Jeeves, in perfect control, counters, "The mood will pass, sir."[161]

The exchanges between master and servant create, for the American reader, a comic confusion. The readers of American literature in the comic tradition have been conditioned and indeed encouraged to equate punch line with the apogee of comic moment. Thus, Jeeves's "the mood will pass, sir," is, for most American readers, the point of humor. This "punch line sensibility" speaks to a peculiarly American need for artistic completion and embodied solution. (The need for completion seems natural enough, as children are encouraged to exult in the resultant four in the addition of two and two. The significant unit, however, is not in the sum, but in the second two. Destination rules the route.) In the dialogue between Bertie and Jeeves, however, the exchange actually reaches its highest comic moment when Bertie retorts, "Do trousers matter?" But comic languages, even among English-speaking cultures, do not always translate well. For example, an English-speaking Hopi Indian takes "look at that wave" and turns it to the more accurate expression, "look at that slash." A wave, after all, is not a singular phenomenon, rather, it is measured in physics and continual motion. In the same way, the American reader's comic sensibility does not, ipso facto, prepare the reader for the language of the English humorists.

Wodehouse has learned his literary lessons, not only from past epochs and comic masters, but from other benign humorists as well. He has, in fact, taken Lewis Carroll's echoing images, de la Mare's "faery flutters," Milne's pristine evocations, and Beatrix Potter's ambivalence, and stripped and redressed them in the crazy quilt of Bertie's glen-plaid confusion. Bertie Wooster, of course, is the deus ex machina by which Wodehouse reveals the alternative language of the benign humorist. The characterization of Bertie Wooster works for Wodehouse in much the same way that the Pooh-bear works for A. A. Milne.

Both Bertie Wooster and Pooh speak a language that precedes and even dictates the flow and action of the stories. Pooh speaks in links of lazy dreams as he shuffles through the grass. Bertie's tongue is moist and hot with unruly rhetoric as he bounds up and over his problems only to have his chin clipped by lowering clouds—puffs that never break open into storm. Where Pooh's language is unassuming and modest, Wooster speaks a highly immodest language; and since action follows language in the works of Milne and Wodehouse, Pooh becomes an answer to the twentieth-century's narcissism while Bertie is narcissism's answer to the twentieth century. Where Pooh drops pebbles in the water to break up the boredom of its placidity, Bertie Wooster chides lakes and streams for rippling just when he wants to look into them to check his cleft and the lay of his marcelled hair.

Both A. A. Milne and P. G. Wodehouse use language which promises to get Pooh, Wooster, and readers off "the eternal hook of life." Wodehouse and Milne tell the critics and readers that if only they will close their critically preconditioned eyes to reopen them to alternative visions, they will begin to *feel* and *sense* a language and literature which catalogues a knut, not with delirium tremens, but with the "shakers" and the "crummies,"—not a Pooh-bear who suffers from adiposity, but one who winningly enjoys a "chubby" existence.

The language of the benign humorists resists superficial scholarship as it continually exhibits a continuity and commonality of purpose which promises a seemingly provocative enjoyment and a "damn good read." But the language is deceptive and subtle as it comes on tip-toes to whisper that it *seems not* to be *what it seems* at all.

The writers of benign literature in nineteenth- and twentieth-century England developed a language that seems filigree but remains difficult to see through. It is a language that rings through itself but leaves no vibrations or traces of sound leading to the literary source of its descriptive richness and euphonic allure. It *is only* what it *is*. In this respect, the language of the benign humorist seemed "unpromising" to such theorists as Benjamin Whorf, who can see "linguistic patterns in serial planes."

In the essay, "Language Mind and Reality," Whorf writes:

> [Language can be like] looking at a wall covered with fine tracery of lacelike design [in which we find] tracery

[which] serves as the ground for a bolder pattern . . . like scrollwork, and that group of scrolls made letters [and] the letters, followed in a proper sequence, made words, the words were aligned in columns which listed and classified entities, and so on in continuing cross-patterning until we found this wall to be a great book of wisdom![162]

The language of such quintessential benign humorists as Milne, Grahame, and Wodehouse, however, never echoes off into metaphor which tracks accuracy and experiential meaning. This is not to say, of course, that the language lacks accuracy and special meaning. Thus, where the Hopi Indian changes "wave" to "slash," the benign humorist changes "the wave bathed the shore" to "the wave sloshed the shore"—something just short of prophetic communication as twentieth-century man and woman know the danger of dipping toes in ecologically imbalanced waters which "slosh" litter on the sand. Indeed, accuracy is not unimportant to the humorists. And after sitting down to a sea-food dinner of scallops, A. A. Milne was asked what he had to eat. Milne correctly replied that he had eaten "a scallop." For the benign humorist, one scallop was just like another; and the fact that they kept coming did not alter their rather singular taste and appeal.

Considerations of a Language-In-Place

Milne, Wodehouse, and Kenneth Grahame close off from the "hoi polloi" of critics and academics new and alternative language which creates not only new literary humours, but innovative, linguistic terrains as well. Their world-as-language is lunatic and real, chic and plebian, and simply confounding. Grahame's Rats, Toads, and Moles; Milne's Bears and Robins; and Wodehouse's Bertie Wooster and Bongo Twistleton-Twistletons, speak a language which creates—almost as it is spoken—lands with blue lawns, tangerine trees, and lollipop houses. Even though the worlds-in-language seem to be miniature and fantastic, the stories and verses which hide in the grass, inside honeycombs and behind ivy walls, are more than precious places where rain falls on roses and whiskers grow on kittens. Inside the language, the Toad, Pooh, and Bertie see "efferything."

Kenneth Grahame's Water Rat perhaps knows something of pantheistic rapport when he speaks to the Mole, "It's [the river] brother and sister to me, and aunts, and company, and food and drink, and (naturally) washing. It's my world, and I don't want any other."[163] Milne's self-effacing Eeyore looks in the river and sees his life given meaning in a ripple and a winkle of water. Amidst the "tra-la-la's" and the "tum-tum-tums," Milne's Pooh knows that the whole cosmos "resides" just outside the hedge. For Pooh, the cosmos is embraceable as Milne's Grand Surveyor brings his language into harmony with the universe. Indeed, Pooh sees the "oneness of things" in his poem:

> How sweet to be a cloud
>   Floating in the Blue!
> Every little cloud
> Always sings loud.
>
> How sweet to be a Cloud
>   Floating in the Blue!
> It makes him very proud
> To be a little cloud.[164]

For Milne and Grahame, nature is the animal's furniture—every cloud is a chair, every rain is a bath, and every sun offers a towel.

Wodehouse, through the character of Bertie Wooster, creates a language of Edwardian and Georgian dimension as the fop hangs his *chapeau* on the elegant hat racks of rusticating homes which, by the twentieth century, more ditted than dotted the Surrey, Sussex, and Shropshire countrysides. The racks stand dry in the corners of rooms which levitate on Oriental rugs, wet and buckling from moisture seeping through roofs above the heads of the twentieth-century's vanishing peerage. But for Bertie Wooster (and one suspects for Wodehouse as well, although he has never been explicit about his feelings for the nobility in England), peerage will always be more important than seepage. Much of Wooster's linguistic world is materialized in aimless travels about the "metrop" and long hours logged in at the "Drones Club." It is inside the "Drones" where Bertie and Reggie, Pongo and Ronny, Horry and Gussie mouth the puppy-speak which piddles down their vests as they laze about in a sublime state of guileless inhibition. By mid-afternoon Bertie and friends tipple and nod off in deep leather chairs aimed at frosted windows which purposely obscure the citizenry and traffic without. The Drones-as-universe offers what Wooster needs to continue his travails across the Empire, smiles, smoke, and billowing bull.

In Kenneth Grahame's *The Wind in The Willows,* language-as-world is found lying about river banks and inside forest-digs. The author's terribly pedestrian-sounding Rats, Moles, Toads, and ferrets join "dabchicks" and "moor-hens" which "cloop" into the crystalline water for a bathe. This land of language, so enchanting yet real, is sensuously threaded with elements making the animals live, warm, and tranquil. Grahame's warm language in *The Wind in the Willows* is similar to Milne's language in the Pooh-books and Wodehouse's Woosterese. The language *is* the environment rather than that which reports and describes it. The language of Grahame, Milne, and Wodehouse is more than mimetic tourism.

It is more than rhetoric for rhetoric's sake to say that the language of A. A. Milne is most artful when seeming to be most simple and unaccomplished. Milne, however, has suffered critical assaults on his benign stories about "simple animals." While it is clever, contemporary criticism has delivered its cruelties. F. C. Crews, for example, in his book *The Pooh Perplex,* scores serious consideration of Milne's books by singling out Proustian interpretations of Milne's Pooh stories which he sees as nothing more than *a la recherche du temps pooh perdu.*[165] Of course, Crews's book is all in fun, and rather full of itself.

Milne's language reveals that animals can be elegant and
graceful, even while living a pristine life based on primitive in-
tuitions and good intentions. There seems nothing more civil-
ized than Pooh's simple life—unfettered by culture—in which the
bear lives in the elegant loveliness of a slow dream. Civility in
Pooh's land is found in quiet, half-stops in "Golden Days" and
in the tasteful indolence of lying in meadows. Milne, however,
does not overcultivate the elegant simplicity of his animal's benign lives. He is artist enough to realize that innocence is best
rendered if juxtapositioned with the not-so-innocent elements in-
frequently found in the "Hundred Acre Wood." But Milne's am-
biguities are of short duration. Thus, when the Pooh-bear asks
Rabbit about access to the Hare's home, Rabbit hints at the
problems of security: "You know how it is in the Forest. One
can't have *anybody* coming into one's house. One has to be
careful." But Rabbit cannot concern himself for long as he is
distracted and asks Pooh, "What about a mouthful of something!"[166] Milne, therefore, does not let ambiguity overstay
as he spirits it away into innocent simplicities and felicitations.

Milne's language has a lyrical simplicity and its sole *raison
d'etre* seems to be to echo off and evaporate into the dew of the
woods, bark into healthy trees, and whisper into the very special grasses which catch it. The language is Aladdin-like. When
Pooh bruises, his "ouches" are turned into echoing and sonorous "owwwess." All is "galoptious" for "Winnie ther Pooh."
"Expeditions" are all "expotitions," and an "ambush" is
merely a "sort of surprise." Kanga's child is named, appropriately enough, "Roo; and , F. C. Crews to the contrary,
Milne must certainly have mulled over the phrase "Helpful
Bear" before deciding to write "Helping Bear." Certainly,
Milne realized that "Helping Bear" gives Pooh a sense of *con-
tinuous* charity.

The Anti-Metaphor in Benign Humor

The language of the humorists feeds anti-metaphorically and incestuously off itself. It is a language that speaks to a philosophy which says profoundly that one equals one and that is enough. The literature of the benign humorist offers the joys of traveling—an enjoyment of trip rather than destination. It is a literary trip not needing the benefit of critical maps and literary cartographers. In this regard, Crews is correct when he writes that it is energetic but "ludicrous" for critics and literary scholars to look for Homeric Myth and Orphic Deism in stories of Milne. So when Pooh climbs trees, holds rallies on hills and clouds, when Bertie Wooster climbs into jumping-jitneys and onto asexual mattresses, and when the Toad in Kenneth Grahame's *The Wind in the Willows* escalates the immodesty of his own personality, the uplift, the traverse, is all in the "climb" as "climb" leads to nothing but the climb itself.

It would be a curious, if false logic to conclude that the literature of such accomplished humorists as A. A. Milne, Kenneth Grahame, and P. G. Wodehouse is *less serious* and *more obscure* than the literature of tragedians, quest novelists, writers of dark-comedy, and the like. For example, at a seminar held at Boston University where escape literature was being discussed, one of the participants, referring to writers of benign humor as well as writers of escape such as Dorothy Sayers and Arthur Conan Doyle, offered that the language and literature of such writers lacked sense *as she knew sense to be*. (Such unstudied postulating is not, of course, much different from scientific theses which conclude that "human beings" live only on "Earth" since the climactic and environmental conditions of other planets will not support what scientists call "human life." More parochial "proof" is offered by those scientists who insist that no life exists elsewhere in the solar system since they haven't seen or heard of any. Such theorizing, of course, is perfect proof that humor resides nowhere and everywhere, even in unsmiling sciences. But "science" remains just what "earthlings" say it is. It is "proven out" by "earthy" postulates and "earthy" experiential data and subsequent empirical testing. But such postulating, testing, and "proofing" is based on data assembled on earth—data which are then presumptively and inappropriately extended to apply to other planets, other galaxies, other universes. Such *metaphorical* erudition shows humor of the highest sort.)

A reader who concludes that humorists such as A. A. Milne, Kenneth Grahame, and P. G. Wodehouse are less worthy of literary esteem, less serious in terms of their language, may also conclude that Beethoven's music is "rather good."

7.
Dimensions of Escape in Benign Humor

It has been traditionally thought that psychotherapies (in all stripes and coloration), transactional analyses, encounter groupings, Freudian meta-speaks, etc. are the most acceptable ways with which to deal with the neuroses besetting a Western people suffering from cultural malaise, societal tremors, and techno-overkill. Traditional therapies have attempted to answer the questions of neuroses such as the attendant problems of the twentieth-century trinity of sex—hetero, homo, and permissive. Too often, traditional approaches to therapy have subscribed to methodologies which attempt to "help" patients (really "impatients" if one considers the persons wanting to get well as soon as possible) by forcing them to confront their problems (i.e. the "reality of it all") and advising them not to try to "escape" from them. Certainly this does not seem to be the best advice possible. After all, if twentieth-century man and woman can "escape" and can remain healthy enough to "escape" another time, another day, by all means "escape."

Many psychiatrists, psychologists, and others in "supportive" mental-health disciplines cavil about and deny the concept of escape. Their denial is accompanied by cautions against escaping— cautions indicating the weak and even cowardly aspects of attempted, psychological escapes. What they actually mean, of course, is that not to face one's problems is somehow analogous to being antisocial, "against society." But even the most ardent critics of escape would have to admit that intellectual escape is a victimless crime.

It is possible, in a purposely non-philosophical way, to cite a syllogism which helps free the concept of escape from its therapeutic designation as an "antisocial behaviorism."

A. anything, device or means by which one can unburden oneself of problems, anxieties, trauma, et al., is beneficial when applied in such a way that no one suffers from the application.

B. "escapism" can be a means and a device by which one can put distance between oneself and problems, anxieties, and trauma without bearing on the conditions of others.

therefore

C. "escapism" is "therapeutically" beneficial when applied properly.

Of course, critics of escape literature also find fault with *where* a reader escapes *to*. But such critics are, in the main, ill-equipped to criticize the *route* of escape since it is a topography which remains hushed, even silent and unavailable to those not in sympathy with the original escape. (It is not gratuitous when viewing the critical problems attending the literature and the literary confusion over *route* and *destination* to consider extra-literary analogies. Wearing yellow pants, a velveteen shirt, and a Pucci scarf about his neck, a Boston student passed two middle-aged men whereupon one man turned to his companion and remarked, "Christ, did you see that fag's clothes?" For the two men, the inference of homosexuality was implicit, not in the college student, but in his clothes. Such criticism, of course, is enervating and rather boring. After all, there is nothing, in and of themselves, homosexually "suggestive" about yellow pants, velveteen shirts, and Pucci scarves. The pants, or course, were doubly victimized in this case by an unfortunate fitting. Similarly, "heroin" is not the problem of addiction; rather, it is the action of the person putting the substance into his or her bloodstream which is the problem. The match, the spoon, the hypodermic are all quite innocent until galvanized by the addict.)

For many, the concept of literary escape is associated with both a literature lacking in a certain seriousness and accomplishment, and with what are considered to be tasteless reading habits. Indeed, the reading of escape literature has been thought to be the exercise of the reader who will not insist on high standards of literary expression. In ways not dissimilar to the thinking expressed by the before mentioned therapist and patient, the literature of escape has been compared to the indulgence of the *unreal* as well as the expression of a desire not to confront the realities of the twentieth-century novel. But for many readers devoted to escape literature, what is *unreal* is the reality of the extra-literary hours they must plug in between literary escapes. In the late nineteenth and early twentieth centuries, however, benign humor promised not only escape, but artistry as well.

Before discussing how the literature of the benign humorists may be directly *utilized* for escape, it is important to reiterate the ways in which the language and literature must be considered. It has been established that traditional forms of literary criticism are often not equal to the task of analyzing the literature of the benign humorist. It is necessary, therefore, to consider new methodologies that will tolerate the unsteadiness of literary criteria and account for the nuances of alternative language used by benign humorists. Critical methodologies, however, are hard to come by and not easily accepted.

David Daiches points to part of the reason why many academics tend to *Pu Pooh Perdu* the literature of the benign humorists, by indicating the pressure academics feel to produce more and more critical works "than they are [generally] interested in and on topics that they are not genuinely 'inward with'."[167] To be "inward with" is to understand the lay of "inscapes" and the play of "inner-weather." Many critics, rightly or wrongly, prefer to keep distance between themselves and the literature under critique. Consequently, many critics are uncomfortable with a literature that demands empathy and a bit of affection.

The benign humorists *write* lands which are alien and attractive, and which have more than a geographic appeal for the twentieth-century person caught in its demographic and societal morass. The humorists offer alternative *visits* to rusticating castles, green and pink hills, and mirrored valleys. It is a land where brooks settle their own reflection, forever, and where forest universes, fields, and meadows go "hummocky" and calm. The environmental inscapes of the humorists offer utopian worlds where Poohbears, Robins, raffish Moles, and rattling Woosters float through lives weaned on constant sunlight and matured in youth.

For the more cynical and infrequent reader of the benign humorists, everything in the literature seems rather impossible. But a first reading, judiciously done, or a discreet rereading, allows the reader to enjoy the laze of making his or her way along streaming new language—a language which would have, if it hadn't gone unnoticed by many readers and educators, already established itself as a *donnee,* an alternative literature not hung on hooks of sociology and darkening literary forms finding expression in dark comedies, bohemian verse, hard novels, and thinly-veiled Babbitries.

A careful reading of the benign humorists indicates the acute instincts by which Milne, Potter, Grahame, and Wodehouse's animals and knuts attain harmonious consonance with "escapist" terrains where new readers find clandestine constellations, with suns and moons which rise and fall in gay obedience to the more haphazard, hence, surer laws of the universe.

Indeed, it is instinct and unsure territory that makes nineteenth and twentieth century humorists preeminently attractive and devoutly hopeful. It is not surprising that the literature offers an almost extra-literary escape by which the twentieth-century reader can temporarily defer the nag and pull of tough living.

Benign Humor: Escape Types

Before discussing the escape potential of the literature, it is necessary to determine the conditioned biases of "adult" readers who would find it less than sophisticated to read and *actually enjoy* such books as Milne's *Winnie the Pooh* and Kenneth Grahame's *The Wind in The Willows.* Milne's Pooh-stories have been relegated to children's libraries and given the precious, critical treatment reserved for "kiddy-lit." "Adult" readers are hesitant to read any book which, simultaneously, can be read by "children." But even for those more unrelenting readers who covet the image of "adulthood," the literature of Milne can be, and should be, read in ways that differ from the reading of the literature by their children. For the adult reader, however, the task of alternative reading is fraught with problems—complexities implicit in the language of the literature, as well as in the book's typography and means of production.

Many of the books of the benign humorists are slim, as even the accomplished humorists realized that innocence and entertainment would not carry long. As a result, the less sophisticated reader who, by the twentieth century, had become curiously conditioned to see the *size* of a book as an indication of its "seriousness," was equally conditioned to "see" the worth of literature in terms of its bulk or lack thereof. This influence, of course, continues to be subtle and almost unwitting. In addition to the influence of size, the more sophisticated reader continues to be disconcerted by such tangential considerations as use of illustrations, graphics, and the need for "white-space."

Undeniably, the illustrations of E. H. Shepard which accompany the text of A. A. Milne's Pooh-books (especially *Winnie the Pooh* and *The House at Pooh Corner*) play more than a complementary role. Indeed, Shepard's illustrations insure the benignity of Milne's language as they realize the grace, innocence, and chuckle-headedness of Pooh and his friends. The illustrations are, in their simplistic way, manifestly gentle as Pooh is delightfully depicted as a brown to beige roll of fur. Shepard's Pooh is the round and constant bruin. But perhaps the most interesting and edifying example of the contribution of Shepard's illustrations to Milne's books is the character Christopher Robin. Milne was aware of the consequences of gender in his Pooh-books; and since the animals are extraordinarily genderless, he realized that Christopher Robin (Pooh's best friend and loosely based on Milne's own son) if drawn boyishly or girlishly would be too jarring an intrusion into a land asexually created and recollected in tranquility and grace. As a result of Milne's wish for "total asexuality," Shepard's Christopher Robin is more buttercup than boy as its hair sparkles golden above faintly boyish, but slightly girlish clothing.

The use of white-space in children's literature is significant. An *increase* of white-space (that part of a page which is print and graphic-free) tends to *decrease,* in the estimation of many readers, the "weight," the significance of the literature. In a curious way, the amount of print on a page helps influence a reader's apprehension of the literature itself. Books whose pages include illustrations, wide margins and a less than average amount of print are inevitably thought to be "less serious" as works of literature than those books which are graphic-free and crammed with print within narrow margins. It is something of a typographical irony that increased white-space, which serves to set off and draw attention to the print within it, also diminishes the impact of the written words.

A. A. Milne: Escape to

Once literary biases are slackened and mollified, and once a certain empathy to the literature is established—uninhibited by extraneous considerations of illustration and typographical nuance—the reader finds that the benign humorists offer something more than just good reading.

For the willing reader, there is something therapeutic in the literary escape offered by the nineteenth- and twentieth-century humorists. But to understand the elements of escape, the reader of benign literature must determine how the literary escape is engineered, where it originates and where it leads. The reader should also consider how such elements of literary escape can be helpful in an extra-literary way. Such attempted determinations, even if unsuccessful, reveal escape routes which are antic and alice, adrift and sliding on the pleasures of good humor.

It is easy enough to *read about* the perpetual light that shimmers down on Milne's Pooh and his dappled and downy friends, and the taste of the dumplings, sweet-meats, and Yorkshire pudding all settled in warm, wicker baskets. But the reader who desires to "escape" *with* and *into* the literature is confronted with certain problems. For example, the reader must not be so concerned with the delightful knowledge that there are traces of Falstaff and Don Quixote in Pooh, as with the realization that the Pooh-bear *seems* formed out of kisses, bubbles, taffy, ribbons, ivory-tipped paws, and velveteen and satin coats—coats which never shed and always stem the moulting period. If the reader finds it difficult to *see* Pooh as Milne imagined him, it is not because the writer's description is ambiguously rendered, but because many adult readers have difficulty in deciding whether or not it is even important to see Pooh at all. For such readers, the literature is grizzly enough.

The route of escape is *through* the Pooh-stories—stories which have the ineffable pull of a simple dream. The tug, however, is in ribbons. In Milne's Pooh-land, there is none of the mysticism of Carroll's rivers and only bare traces of the shivering enchantments populating Grahame's wild wood and forests, as Pooh lives beneath white clouds which puff about the trees and drape away the *without*. The benign clouds decorate the sky and filter the sun which, in Milne's stories, acts as more than a predictor of weather and an encouragement to Ektachrome. All of Pooh's balloons rise toward the sun, while in the *without* only those helium-filled "can get up for it."

Before escape the reader must acquire a taste and develop a feel for a land which has been milked and honeyed by Milne, and has been arranged by his deus ex machina to be "neat" and "clean" and "nice." But Milne's world is not so much chimerical as it is visionary.

Kenneth Grahame: Escape into

A more complex escape route is found in the geography of euphonics so stunningly deployed by Kenneth Grahame in his masterpiece *The Wind in the Willows*. The language of *Willows* is extraordinary when read, but when read aloud, it is magical. Grahame's language is a torrent of textures, smells, and sounds that pile and drift in sensuous geometrics when placed into air. The reader-as-hearer gets a feel for the material properties of the language. Although the language seems too perfumed at times, too descriptively indulgent and fragrant, the empathetic reader needs to know the *The Wind in The Willows* better. Grahame's story offers an escape to a place filled with yams, carrots, and peas which stew in pots that scald smilingly atop red hearths. It is a place of charmed rooms where well-loomed rugs lay beneath bully-boyed tables and Chippendale that isn't. *Willows* catalogs yellow suns, blue-blisses, and crackling airs—airs which carry the smell of honey and milk to fussy animals and "leaping pike." On the ground, all the beasts are bricks to each other, and any bellicosity soon airs out in lavender clouds. All problems in Grahame's *The Wind in The Willows* are spirited away short of trouble.

The Wind in The Willows, through the sheer intensity of its descriptive passages, is more escapist than Milne's Pooh-books in that Grahame's book lends itself effectively, and most appropriately, to the oral tradition in literature. Thus, Willows offers the dimension of auditory space as the air is filled with intoxications of language which fall on the ears with such vitality that each sentence seems an epiphany. When read aloud, therefore, *The Wind in The Willows* creates a heightened awareness of the language as the listener hears the range and flow of sounds which, if continued to the printed page, would have only the inner ear to distinguish it. This is not to imply that Grahame's *Willows* is unsuccessful as printed literature. It is a testimony to the writer's artistry that his book remains a masterpiece of the oral and written traditions of English literature. It is equally apparent, however, that to hear ". . . little lawn of a marvellous green, set round with Nature's own orchard trees—crab apple, wild cherry and sloe," is not to want to read it.[168] Indeed, the escape route encouraged by *The Wind in the Willows* leads into the sounds of its language.

P. G. Wodehouse: Escape towards Life-Style

P. G. Wodehouse's Bertie Wooster-Jeeves short stories and novels offer a different escape route from those offered by Milne and Grahame. This escape is not *to* a land (Milne) or *into* a place-as-language (Grahame), rather, it is *towards* a life-style. Bertie Wooster's life-style is modeled after the post-Edwardian, slip-away peerage, and knuttery. Unlike *The Wind in the Willows,* the Wooster-Jeeves books chronicle a life-style best seen in the spilling-about-the-page of language which describes the foppish Bertie. Wodehouse's stories, although curiously lyrical and poetic, will not support themselves in language alone. Thus Wodehouse sees that even the punctuation marking the exchanges between Bertie and his valet Jeeves seems significant. Exclamation points (a "printing crutch" which Wodehouse usually abhorred) are used judiciously in order to indicate perpetually puzzled and feverishly knitting brows. Wodehouse, delightfully designing, uses commas with purpose. When Jeeves asks Bertie "How do you feel, sir?" the reader, hearing the line uttered aloud, suspects that Jeeves is, perhaps, slightly less than concerned with the answer. Indeed the emphasis is on the words "how" and "sir," with the result that the valet seems insincere or, at least, "uffish." When the line is read, however, the question is artfully and rather coyly ambiguous.

The reader of Wodehouse's Bertie-Jeeves saga wants to know more about Wooster's hedonistic way with life as the knut struts, preens, and trips through halcyon days. (It is more than a curious analogy that where English literature gives us the daily life-style escape of the ultimate Wooster, American audiences opted for the not dissimilar life-stylings of Ozzie Nelson of the "Ozzie and Harriet" television series. Wooster is not unlike the bumbler Nelson as both fops have no means of support, are "bonkers" about ice-cream and know the splendid dimensions of dither.) Bertie Wooster's life-style is steps beyond eccentricity. The young master is lazy and indolent, mentally dwarfed, tippled, and drunken. Wodehouse's knut is an ethical nondescript and a moral brigand. He wears it all rather well, however, and even his clothes do much to help out "the old image." His body is tweeded and herringboned, and his alligator shoes are "crocked." But to the twentieth century reader of the Wooster-Jeeves saga Wooster's life-style is all *just right* since it's all so obviously antisocial and seemingly wrong.

So intoxicating is Wodehouse's character Bertie Wooster, that an elderly and engaging iconoclast named Helen Sherman Miller started what she and other Wodehousians called "Bertie Wooster Clubs Ltd." after reading and rereading the entire Wooster-Jeeves cycle of stories five times. During a meeting of the "Bertie Wooster Club" where the joys of a Woosterian life were discussed, Miller offered that anyone, if given the choice, would like to "drink the hours away," without what the assertive Miller called the "dits," "slurs," and "crummies." (Before her death, Helen Miller claimed to have prepared herself for Wodehouse's literature by reading Proust's *Swann's Way* three times.)

Escape Language

Kenneth Grahame offers a world-in-language *into* which one might escape, A. A. Milne offers a paradisical land *to* which one might escape, and P. G. Wodehouse develops a lifestyle which *is* the very essence of escape. It matters little whether the literature of escape of the late nineteenth- and early twentieth-century benign humorists is *into, to* or *towards;* the common denominator that influences and engineers the escape is the consummate use of what shall be called escape language.

When assessing the literature of the humorists in terms of escape-potential, the reader must consider what for most of the humorists amounts to a literary truism—that every *thing* in the stories is a letter, letters grouped, words and sentences. Only the letters t-h-i-n-g *is a "thing."* Pooh-lands, Toad Hall, The Drones, Croquet lawns, rabbit holes, et al., are places which are only manifest in terms of letters and words which describe and, consequently, attend and maintain them. Therefore, the escape offered by the literature is *into, to* and *towards* language. The language is the very quiddity of matter, a "matter" which George Steiner in his book *Extraterritorial Papers on Literature and the Language of Revolution* calls "extraterritorial." Not surprisingly, the "extraterritorial" matter (language) is more easily appreciated by the less sophisticated reader since the more highly literate reader tends to "overcultivate" and index the language of such humorists as Milne, Grahame, and Wodehouse, thus removing it from its contextual pristine state in the literature. Benign humor, as a result, is less satisfying as escape literature for the "sophisticated" reader who has difficulty shedding literary predilections and metaphorical conclusions. (It is this same reader, however, who wants to disbelieve that bees dance their messages to each other, refuses to admit dolphins are canny, and continually denies that Humpback Whales sing electronic arias.) The language of the benign humorists does not reward the overly analytical reader. But because the language feasts on risible phrases which glissade down "moon-mad" banks, the reader must not conclude that it lacks complexity and nuance.

Preconditions of Escape

When reading the literature of the benign-humorists for escape, it is necessary to recognize that simplicity of expression—incidence of familiar words—is not an indication, in and of itself, that the language lacks literary dimension and means of artful communication. (It is significant, perhaps, that despite the existence of over 600,000 words in the English language there are fewer than a hundred which account for most telephone and telegraphic messages.) The humorists, in fact, do not even think of the words "simplicity" and "communication" in the same way that the more traditional writers and critics think of them. For the English humorists, "simplicity" means "identification" whereas "communication" means "empathy."

The concept of literary empathy must be examined closely. This does not mean, however, that the reader wishing to read Kenneth Grahame's *The Wind in The Willows* for its escape potential must be intoxicated and immersed in its language. The empathy necessary to reading the literature of Grahame, Milne, and Wodehouse is manifest in reader's identification of the literature as writing that calls for an almost total concentration. (A Michigan State University team of parapsychologists and graduate students in psychology headed by Hugh David Bordinat has done research into the question of concentration in terms of its positive and negative effects on the accomplishing of successful, therapeutic sessions. Of significant interest to the group was the question of a phenomenon commonly called "white noise." Using literature, the test group found that white-noise, which is commonly thought to be the *sound* of *non-sound*— a hearable silence which seems to preempt more identifiable noise—disrupts and destroys the concentration of patients. Bordinat found that such noises as traffic flow, car horns, birds singing, doors shutting, etc., are in a noise-polluted era no longer thought of and apprehended as noise since they have become so familiar and integrated. When such common noises were concealed or eliminated, and then substituted with quiet, the resultant white-noise appeared to inhibit concentration. Although such research is admittedly inconclusive it is not lacking in a certain whimsicality.).

The reader of the benign humorists, wishing to use the literature for escape, must also be conscious of being unconscious of the material presentation of the literature. Besides consideration of illustrations, white space, etc., the reader must first consider then dismiss the effect on the literature of paperback book presentation. George Steiner is correct when he theorizes that there is, about the paperback book, something "designedly ephemeral." For Steiner, one reason for reading a paperback book is an attempt to "conquer and defeat time."[169] Generally speaking, reading a paperback book arrests time since thinking about time seems less important. When reading paperbacks, time doesn't pass and it doesn't *not* pass. Still, such reading seems too fleeting an experience. The very flexibility of the book (its lightness and material malleability) seems to make its reading *less* significant a pursuit. Instead, the book itself seems to hold a stopwatch on the reader asking him to get on with it. While reading a hardcover book, on the other hand, the reading experience itself seems somehow less pedestrian. It is not surprising, therefore, that Wodehouse's critical stock has not risen despite new issuances of his books in paper. Milne's Pooh-stories, Beatrix Potter's squirrely tales, and Kenneth Grahame's *The Wind in The Willows*, however, also have been reissued in various hardcover editions.

Thus the literature of the English benign humorists, if read for escape, must be isolated from the uninformed labels publishers and libraries fix to the literature such as children's literature, "childhood fantasies," etc. The reader who wishes to exercise the implicit, escape potential in the work of the humorists must recognize that the escape implicit in the works of all the benign humorists, from Lewis Carroll to P. G. Wodehouse, is in its *route,* not its *destination.*

Benign Humor As Escape Destination and Route

Properly predisposed, in the proper setting, and with the literature properly presented, the reader of the literature of the humorists need only recognize the reading experience itself as the escape. The readings are brief—Milne's Pooh-stories, Grahame's *Willows,* and Wodehouse's shorter novels take an average reader one to two hours to read—and the reader must know that the escape is all along the route, engineered by and within the language. The "escapee" must recognize the terrain of language. To understand the language is to have a "spirit of place."

Milne's Pooh-land is bound by both time and space. In the 1957 edition of *Winnie the Pooh,* the inside front cover depicts the land and its immediate environs. In the E. H. Shepard illustration, there appears the small but imposing "Hundred Acre Wood." To enhance the possibility of escape, Milne and Shepard were aware that things (language) had to appear (therefore *be*) benign, innocent, fulfilled. In this way, the "Hundred Acre Wood" satisfies in a way precluded to the reader confronted by a Ninety-Nine Acre Wood or a Hundred and one Acre Wood. Such considerations, although seemingly fatuous, bear out. Shepard's illustration at the beginning of *The World of Pooh* runs tight to the edges of the book's margins. At the periphery of Milne's land (and the book cover), Shepard draws (with words alone, but a *draw,* nevertheless) such "nowhere" places as North Pole, Floody Place, and Rather Boggy and Sad. Shepard's intention is clear as his illustration encourages the reader to dismiss the *possible* lands extant, while it secures and demystifies the land.

A. A. Milne's land—the place of escape—is tranquil and Edenic. It is a place—a language—where small flusters and pieces of animal business take place. Milne's locale sports words which turn into "Hums." By the iconic simplicity of the words and the symbolic emptiness of "Hums," Milne discourages metaphorical linkages to the world *without* by using language that not only *describes* the place but *is* the place. Milne's language in the Pooh-stories *is* and engineers the escape.

In *the House at Pooh Corner,* the escape dies as Christopher Robin feels "the pull of reality"—a force he feels "might lead to something." Christopher Robin tells his friend Edward Pooh Bear that he (Christopher Robin) is "not going to do nothing any more." For the empathetic reader, the considerable logic of the line is clear; and if the reader properly prepares for the possibility of escape, he realizes that it is unproductive to understand how words might fold into other words which are, after all, merely forest creases. The prepared reader realizes that Milne's lavender clouds and fluffs of heather are "growed-up" words that predispose the reader to accept the ache of escape as Milne engages the bear and his friends, the readers, with tugging hearts. It is the "ache," of course, that lets the reader know that he or she has escaped. If the sensitive reader is distressed by the conclusion to Milne's *The House At Pooh Corner,* it is but one way in which the effectiveness and completeness of the escape is measured. At the end of *Pooh Corner,* "Factors" must bear. Reality weighs. The escape is concluded.

The escape offered by Kenneth Grahame's *The Wind in the Willows* is both more and less difficult than the escape made possible by the literature of A. A. Milne. As mentioned before, the literary escape of *The Wind in the Willows* is simplified by an oral presentation of the classic, but, at the same time, the escape is bound to the language *into* which the escape takes place. Unlike Milne's stories where things (words) *point to* a land of similar language which also seems familiar in an abstract, geographic sense, Grahame's words and places have a faint unthreatening supernatural quality as the writer outwrites "River Banks" and "Enchanted Forests."

The Wind in the Willows, of course, offers an escape possible to any reader who finds release in the mere reading of good literature. In this way all literatures are *potentially* escapist. But, as with almost all the literature of the benign humorists, there is the escape within the escape in Grahame's classic work. *The Wind in the Willows* blows through an "extraterritorial" language which demands that the escaping reader "connect to" the swell of the story's acoustics and the play of its phonetics. Through the richness of its language, Grahame's story forces the reader to take account of the material properties and dimensions of words which seem to form in the wind, expand in the air. And while many of the simple words populating Milne's Pooh-stories can be viewed as adjunctive to the stories themselves, Kenneth Grahame's *The Wind in the Willows* forces the reader to encounter each sound, individually and alone.

Indeed, *The Wind in the Willows* is an escape "INTO" "into-ness," a linguistic probe of the "within the without." To understand this, of course, is not to be so repelled by the vernacular of some youth when they utter "I'm really into the [Rolling] Stones'" or "I'm really into my studies now," (the latter expression, of course, is less frequently used.) Indeed, the "into-ness" of these lines suggest an "out-of-ness"—an escape. The INTO-ness of *the Wind in the Willows* is a euphonically engineered miracle—a miracle made possible by the oral tradition in literature.

P. G. Wodehouse's Bertie Wooster-Jeeves short stories and novels offer a literary escape decidedly less satisfying and less complete than those encouraged by Milne's *Winnie the Pooh* and *The House at Pooh Corner* and Kenneth Grahame's *The Wind in the Willows*. One of the reasons is that Wodehouse's language—discreet borrowings from and bastardization of traditional usages—lacks the seminal and iconic quality of the language born and bred in the Alice books, the Pooh-stories, and Grahame's classic. Wodehouse's language, although seemingly invented in the mouth of Wooster, is rooted in different languages and literary traditions. It is Edwardian; it is Elizabethan; it is Georgian; it is farcical. But when combined artfully and confined to the Wooster-Jeeves *oeuvre,* it is quite Wodehousian.

Although the language is less imaginative, Wodehouse's Wooster-Jeeves saga, like the Pooh-books and *Wind in the Willows,* indicates that the escape of benign humor is all in the route as it denies destination which is always out of reach *exactly where it isn't*. The *route* of escape is out from Bertie Wooster's blueberry lips and into a life-style which promises the knut a pleasant but early death. So where the escape *is* the language in Kenneth Grahame's *The Wind in the Willows,* the escape offered by Wodehouse's literature is manifest in a way of life expressed by language. The escape, therefore, is once removed from the language. This does not suggest, however, that the Wodehouse qua Wooster escape is any less possible or rewarding if considered properly.

Character empathy is encouraged and easier in the literature of P. G. Wodehouse since the reader suspects that there is something elusive but quite real in Bertie Wooster. The reader who sees the characterization of Bertie Wooster as real, however, is actually bespeaking a desire to make it real. Wodehouse's Wooster, after all, has a "crackling" and "tinkerty-tonk" good thing. His life is a succession of sensuous days and bizarre nights into which the dogs don't bark. For the twentieth-century reader, however, imagination is taxed as Wodehouse asks the reader to "get in there" and knock-about the mahogany and feel the leather. To grasp the characterization of Wooster is to exert the imagination in order to smell the "steaming tea" and the tangerine-bobbed hair of Wodehouse's perfumed girls. It is clear that the success of imagination denies the hindrance to escape posed by a life-style that seems fictional.

The key to the "Wooster-escape" is in the sum and not the addition. In fact, there is nothing, if considered separately and singularly, "unreal" about the life-style of Wooster which plays in tweeds, plaids, silver-tipped gaspers, kid-gloves, marcelled hair, and starched collars. What is delightfully "unreal" is that Wooster wears and sports the elements all at one time. In the same way there is nothing incongruous about eggs, bacon, kippers, salmon, tomato juice, and champagne until Bertie indulges in them all at one breakfast sitting. The characterization of Bertie Wooster seems foam-born, an aquaplane in tug days. He is an attractive jujube, flash without brilliance. Bertie is in the constant swim of things but must eventually sink under the weight of too many martinis. Wodehouse's Wooster is a duck who wants a lord's love and a reader's sympathy. Sympathy indicates empathy, and empathy involves the literary escape.

If it is difficult, however, for modern readers to empathize with ponies and roses which get trampled and eaten by stallions and snapdragons, it is easier to identify with a life-style which features the more estimable twentieth-century qualities of ethical sloth, moral ambivalence, lechery, and drunkeness. But even these "qualities" are benignly rendered by Wodehouse. The readers of the Wooster-Jeeves saga, therefore, suspect that they might do worse than lead an existence (if only for two hours or so) long on pleasures and played out under surried skies and shrop-cropped trees. The escape encouraged by the literature of Wodehouse is so bound to a way of life, rather than to language, that the reader of the Wooster-Jeeves saga identifies—empathizes—escapes—with the character of Wooster who is in reality an erratic product of a more predictable language. The language of Wodehouse, therefore, tends to be overlooked. Thus the reader forgets to smell the flowering of the language along the way while viewing the essence of escape within the characterization of Bertie Wooster. The reader who deliberately reads Wodehouse for escapism is frustrated and dissatisfied if he or she deals too explicitly with the characterization of Bertie Wooster. Indeed, Bertie Wooster is an evanescent caricature of a language on the run, rhetoric loudly rioting. In the final analysis Wooster is nothing but a sweep of language. He is a confused life-style measured in a consciously twisted language.

The escape offered by the literature of the benign humorists is not only pleasant in an extra-literary way; it offers methodless ways by which to sense a literature that refuses critical roughhousing. Granted, there are escape elements and escapist potential implicit in almost all literary forms. But the ideal literary escape presumes that the escape will somehow be constructive while offering a congenial experience—if only as a brief respite. The ideal literary escape is best rendered expeditiously, but not so fleetingly that the reader loses the tang of the going. Indeed, such benign humorists as A. A. Milne, Kenneth Grahame, and P. G. Wodehouse offer proof that literary escape in benign literature is all in the food. The literature is more than a healthy repast for its readers, however, and such quintessential benign humorists as Lewis Carroll, Edward Lear, Beatrix Potter, Walter de la Mare, Milne, Grahame, and P. G. Wodehouse knew what Charles Lamb meant when the latter wrote about the function of escape-literature: ". . . [after reading it] I could come back to my cage and my restraint the fresher and more healthy for it."

8.
Benign Humor and Escape Literature

Manifest in the twentieth century are elements and dimensions of both unintentional and intentional literary escape. In addition to the benign humorists, there were the English writers of a literature which remains more intentionally escapist and not as concerned with the specific properties of escape language. The most gifted and consummate writers of this more designing escape literature are Arthur Conan Doyle and Dorothy Sayers.

The escape literature of Conan Doyle's Sherlock Holmes stories and Dorothy Sayers's Lord Peter Wimsey adventures is carefully designed and written with a mathematical precision with which both writers build the momentum of detection—a momentum which more than compensates for the occasionally rambling plot and intriguingly bloated but rich characterizations common to both Sayers and Conan Doyle.

There are significant similarities between the benign humorists and Conan Doyle and Sayers, not the least being critical nonacceptance of their literature. The work of the humorists along with the escape literature of Sayers and Conan Doyle serves not only as an example of the artistry implicit in what many critics cavalierly call light literature but also as a means to study the extent to which literature can be used for artistic escape.

Wodehouse and Conan Doyle: Language and Team

When assessing the "intentional escape" encouraged by the Sherlock Holmes and Doctor Watson stories of Arthur Conan Doyle, it is necessary to see Doyle's work in light of its remarkable similarities to the Bertie Wooster-Jeeves stories of Wodehouse. It is apparent, for example, that Wodehouse found many precedents for his Wooster-Jeeves saga in the Holmes-Watson adventures. Wodehouse, in fact, knows Doyle's stories as well as any Baker Street Irregular. Wodehouse has never denied his admiration for Conan Doyle, and in a 1925 letter to W. H. Townend, the author of the Wooster-Jeeves saga writes:

> I'm having lunch with Conan Doyle. . .
> Conan Doyle, a few words on the subject of. Don't you find as you age-in-the-wood, as we both are doing, that the tragedy of life is that your early heroes lose their glamour. . .?
> Now with Doyle, I don't have this feeling. I still revere his work as much as ever. I used to think it swell, and I still think it swell . . .
> And apart from his work, I admire Doyle so much as a man, I should call him definitely a great man, and I don't imagine that I'm the only one who thinks so. I love that solid, precise way he has of talking like Sherlock Holmes.[170]

Both Wodehouse and Conan Doyle were published in *Strand* before distribution of their Wooster-Jeeves and Holmes-Watson sagas was realized in book form. In fact, it was the arrival of Conan Doyle's Sherlock Holmes adventures that made Dulwich bearable for the "disinterested studier," Wodehouse. In Wodehouse's "public school" novels which include *The Pothunters* (1902), *A Perfect Uncle* (1903), and *The Gold Bat* (1904), there are numerous references to Doyle's *Rodney Stone* and in two of Wodehouse's earlier stories, two public school boys name their pet ferrets after Sir Nigel (from Conan Doyle's *The White Company*). In *Mike at Wrykn,* a young boy refuses to leave his flat to go to the rugby field until his revered copy of Conan Doyle's "The Adventure of the Speckled Band" arrives. Indeed, all the young readers in Wodehouse's early works have a catholic but discriminating teste for literature as they shuffle between the classics, from Dickens to Doyle.

Wodehouse's finest character, Bertie Wooster, often employs a language which seems to have been inspired by the spilling rhetoric of Conan Doyle's Dr. Watson. Both Wooster and Watson juggle colloquialisms and idiom, and none too successfully. Both men wait for some client to "creep up the stairs of Berkely Mansions and 21 Baker Street" to seek a resolution to their problem, not from Wooster and Watson, but from the unlimited resources of Jeeves and Sherlock Holmes. Doctor Watson has the same sense of whimsey that Bertie Wooster has. The bored physician is chocker-full of the same mischievious predilections which attend and whelm Bertie Wooster. Both Wooster and Watson love the intrigue of chase, and throughout the stories which chronicle the adventures of Holmes, Watson slyly alludes to tales he prefers to keep in his fuddled head and, fortunately, in the vault at Cox's at Charing Cross. Where Wooster tells Jeeves "I can't even talk about it," Watson teases the reader with promised stories about "the shocking affair of the Dutch steamship, *Friesland,* the "giant rat of Sumatra," and "the notorious canary-trainer." All Watson will say is that the "world is not yet prepared to hear."

The similarities between the teams are striking. Both teams know the pleasure of opera, sea cruises, and small libations at the Covent Garden. Both Conan Doyle and Wodehouse make outrageous use of hyperbole and missed thoughts. And just as sure as Bertie Wooster is that he can jump into his bed, cozy down into lush muslin sheets, and toss-off a couple of quick chapters of Spinoza and Nietszche, Watson is secure in the classics as he feels no discomfort when strolling in on the *second* act of a Wagnerian Opera.

The similarities between the teams proliferate. While Wooster was known in school as "the bungler," Dr. Watson promises to bungle and undo Holmes's deductive reasonings. Both teams discuss the day's action over "b" and "e" followed by an imminent departure from the "Metrop." The adventures themselves take place in and about baronial homes and rusticating estates. At the end of Conan Doyle and Wodehouse's stories, there is the predictable gathering of all suspects and participants in the adventures, as they line leathery dens to hear what Holmes and Jeeves have to offer. Both Sherlock Holmes and Wooster are practicing misogynists. Bertie Wooster plays with but abhors the fallow dimensions of such free spirits as "Stiffy" Byng, "the Bassett," and that "fish Florence Craye." Sherlock Holmes, on the other hand, has been touched by just one woman. Watson narrates:

> To Sherlock Holmes she is always the woman. I have seldom heard him mention her under any name. . . . All emotions and that one particularly, were abhorrent to his cold, precise, but admirably balanced mind.[171]

Richard Usborne in *Wodehouse at Work,* develops the similarities between Conan Doyle and Wodehouse.

> The Bertie-Jeeves [stories] may be an echo of the Sherlock Holmes stories . . . blackmail, theft, revolver shots in the night, air-guns shot by the day, butlers in dressing gowns, people climbing in at the bedroom windows, people dropping out at the bedroom windows, people hiding in bedroom cupboards, the searching of bedrooms for missing manuscripts, cow-creamers and pigs.[172]

R. B. D. French also sees the similarities betwen Wodehouse and Conan Doyle, but seems less than convinced by them. In a chapter entitled "A Bloke and His Valet," French writes, somewhat reluctantly:

> The whole thing is rather like Sherlock Holmes and Watson, except that Watson rarely interferes with the detective's plans and Bertie horrifies his friends by announcing that he has taken their cases into his own hands.[173]

The difference between the escape *offered* by the life-style of Bertie Wooster and the escape made mandatory with the edge of mystery by Conan Doyle, is manifest in the atmosphere of both Wooster's and Holmes's lodgings. Bertie Wooster's quarters, before the efficient Jeeves makes them liveable by noon, are configurated in the wraps and language of tweed-jackets, red scarves, yellow mittens, and brown mufflers and puffs which pile on, trace and track the floors. Wooster's rooms are filled and littered with the remains of words out-of-synchronization but at home with the knut. Sherlock Holmes's study at Baker Street is more pungent with immaterial atmosphere as gaslights exaggerate the cocaine swirls and violin notes which bounce off furniture and walls, sinisterly pocked by rehearsing bullets. Bertie Wooster's rooms are thick with alcohol and Jeeves's philosophical tracts, while Sherlock Holmes's flat is cluttered with persian slippers filled with tobacco, coal scuttles, and "books of detection."

Where Wodehouse's Wooster is inexplicably simple, Conan Doyle's characterization of Sherlock Holmes is enigmatic as the reader wonders how and why the sleuth maintains a cocaine habit and an aversion to females. (To the latter consideration, Holmes answers, "imprecise thinkers.") Sherlock Holmes's rather Jeevesian appearance is quite unlike Bertie Wooster's and his keen, edged head with the "dead-white tinge of his aquiline face," is totally dissimilar to the pink-cheeked Wooster with his unknit brows and marcelled hair. The similarities between the characters and stories in Wodehouse and Conan Doyle's *oeuvres* are so striking that the contemporary reader is hard pressed to read one without thinking of the other.

Dorothy Sayers: Elegant Resolution

Dorothy Sayers's stories and novels outline and untangle the plots and intrigues which confront the engaging peer-as-sleuth, Lord Peter Wimsey, and are as deliberately escapist as the Sherlockian stories of Conan Doyle. Sayers's stories, however, are more benign, made light and gay by the properly hedonistic

peer. Sayers's Wimsey stories appeal to similar and small
pockets of readers who attempt to keep sacrosanct the rarefied
delights of Conan Doyle and the benign humorists. *Clouds of
Witness* (1926), *The Unpleasantness at the Bellona Club* (1928),
and *The Five Red Herrings* (published in the United States in
1931, not surprisingly, under the title *Suspicious Characters*),
are the works which established the reputation of Sayers in both
England and America.

As it is with the shorter works of Conan Doyle, Sayers's predilection for the literary escape ethos is projected in the titles
of her short stories. In part, it is in the titles where the differences between Sayers's "Wimseys" and Conan Doyle's Holmesian
adventures are first indicated. Conan Doyle's titles, such as "The
Adventure of the Devil's Foot," "The Adventure of the Engineer's
Thumb," "The Adventure of the Red Carbuncle," etc., are more
resplendently mysterious and fraught than Sayers' less malignant
"The Bibulous Business of a Matter of Taste," "The Piscatorial
Farce of the Stolen Stomach," and "The Incredible Elopement of
Lord Peter Wimsey." The playful and sly quality of the titles
correctly indicates that Sayers' adventures of Lord Peter are going
to be stylized tales where manners and taste can apprehend proper
culprits who enact what the reader is encouraged to see as
victimless crimes.

Lord Peter Wimsey is the elegant peer engaged in the "right
sort" of leisures. Wimsey moves from teas to trout streams as
he dogs out murders spread from Sussex to Scotland. Lord Peter
Wimsey practices detection in ways that are appropriately successful and careless. But Wimsey's is a practical carelessness
as Sayers has the peer "droppin" his "g's" and shuffling
"aint's" and "gonnas" into his mellifluous sentences. But
Wimsey is elegantly aloof, and his butler Bunter knows it is in-
excusable to contradict his master's speech—a reserve of service
not practiced by Jeeves who, as grammarian and lexicographer,
will not abide Bertie Wooster's fracturing of language.

The escape implicit in Dorothy Sayers's Lord Peter Wimsey
novels and short stories is as designing as that encouraged by
the Sherlock Holmes stories of Conan Doyle. Both escapes are
quite different from that offered by the benign humorists who

provide a linguistic escape route flowing into nowhere. Dorothy Sayers's stories, on the other hand, dam against mathematical plottings and tie in tangled webs of telling evidence. In fact, Dorothy Sayers, like Conan Doyle, makes few literary concessions to language. But, again like Conan Doyle, Sayers is the consummate mathematician who knows the exact moment for literary *denouement*.

Lord Peter Wimsey is the more benign sleuth; where Sherlock Holmes manifests a monkish life-style based on asceticism and the dogged determination to worship himself, Wimsey is a loving sort, not plagued by any Moriarity, who finds even the culprits whom he apprehends "decent sorts." But Wimsey is a cunning lover, and "when on case" his charm and affecting looks are used as weapons. Indeed, Wimsey is a cross between Sherlock Holmes and Bertie Wooster for the elegant peer always gets his man, but not without hangovers and bruises to his ego.

Dorothy Sayers brought to her writing the eye and analytical mind of a journalist and scholar. And where Conan Doyle practiced medicine while penning the adventures of Holmes—a vocation out of which grows Sherlock Holmes's ability to find symptom, make diagnosis, and offer prognostication—Dorothy Sayers was a diligent scholar. Evidence of her ample scholarship is her interesting translation of Dante's *Divine Comedy*. (The translation of "Hell" appeared in 1949, "Purgatory" in 1955. The translation was completed by Barbara Reynolds, for "Paradise" appeared in 1962 after the death of Sayers. The writer was feverishly engaged in her translation and research of Dante, and in 1954 and 1957 she published two distinguished works, "Introductory Papers on Dante," and "Further Papers on Dante.") But Sayers is the more ingenious writer of detection and escape literature. In her Wimsey stories she is the committed scholar who balances her mind with the puzzles that Lord Peter pieces together. Dorothy Sayers, however, suffers from the same critical disrespectability that attends the benign humorists, and where A. A. Milne attempted serious plays, Sayers wrote scholarly tracts. Although somewhat overstated, James Sandoe in his introduction to the anthology *Lord Peter*

(1972) writes of a Sayers who "wrote ingeniously, wittily and clearly . . . and with as deep a responsibility to the tale of detection as she brought to the tale of salvation while translating Dante."[174]

Dorothy Sayers designed her stories to be escapist. Each Wimsey is a puzzle of human erudition and missed parts. The escape, not dissimilar to that offered by P. G. Wodehouse, is realized through an identification to plot and, especially, character. The plots are as puzzling as the character of Lord Peter as the peer "figgers" it out with a cool precision unexpected from the erratic and seemingly unprepared intelligence of the gentleman sleuth. Wimsey is the "fuddled" tactician who designs the escape implicit in Dorothy Sayers's literature. For Wimsey, as for Sayers, plot solution *is* the escape. In this way, of course, the escape is too acquisitive as the reader must acquiesce and acquire signs, i.e. "clues," which will bring the solution, the escape. The reader of Wimsey who looks ahead to plot resolution, therefore, is disappointed since he or she cannot enjoy "the going," the way to the destination, the escape route.

It matters little whether the concept of literary escape is intentional or a by-product of language; the critics continue to deal harshly with such literature. Critical disdain of the escape literature offered by the benign humorists as well as the more intended escapist fare of such writers as Conan Doyle and Dorothy Sayers, however, is not solely rendered in respect to applied literary criteria; rather, such criticism is the partial product of social and cultural considerations which continue to mitigate against the concept, both literary and otherwise, of escape.

Critical Considerations of Escape Literature

The benign humorists as well as Conan Doyle and Dorothy Sayers have had their literature victimized by a preconditioned distrust of the concept of literary escape. Such critical corn grows out of the historical husk of cultural concern. The problems for writers of escape literature are curiously inherent in a stereotypic, extra-literary dialogue between psychiatrist and patient.

> *Patient* I've got to get away from it all. I don't know what's bothering me, but I've got to get away.
> *Doctor* No! You mustn't do that, you must learn to *face* your *problems.* You can't always take the easy way out. After all you can't escape forever.

The patient, of course, does not know *exactly* what is bothering him, but he *does know* that he *doesn't* what to be troubled by whatever or whomever is doing the troubling. The doctor's reply suggests that he also *doesn't know exactly* what is bothering the patient and he doesn't know what the patient's problems are. He does know, however, that he *doesn't want* the patient *not* to know what his or her problems are. It is less cynical than clear that it is "alleged" problems which bind patient and doctor together. After the patient apprises the psychiatrist that he wants to "get away from it all," essentially wants to *escape,* the doctor sees the proclamation as an indication that the patient's "problems" must be large and fraught, or why else would the patient want to "escape" from them. The more rhetorically gifted clinician, however, might have realized that it is more than sleight-of-hand, linguistic trickery to conclude that if the patient does not *learn* to "face the problems" as defined by the doctor, that he will never recognize the alleged "problems" as "problems" at all. But, of course, "problems" are a currency of the profession as many in the "mind-sciences" have a stake in *materializing* "problems" whenever possible. Certainly, the benign humorists would have enjoyed the logic behind the doctor's statement, "you can't escape forever." The humorist might have asked the doctor how

he or she knows that since obviously they have not tried it successfully.

Many literary critics and academic scholars have let similar
considerations, extrinsic and foreign to any positive literary
criteria, color their criticism of the literature of escape. For
example, Sylvan Barnet, Morton Berman, and William Burto,
in their book, *The Study of Literature,* define "escape literature" as "writing designed to allow the reader to forget the
cares of this life while [entering] a 'never-never land' or
'outer-space.'" They conclude that "such writing presumably
gratifies the reader's fantasies, and thus may serve a useful
purpose."[175] Of significance is the use by Barnet, Berman,
and Burto, of conditional words such as "presumably," and
"may." Such use suggests a rhetorical hedging against the
possibility that the reader, and especially academic colleagues,
might think that they (Barnet, Berman and Burto) have actually
read any escape literature. In addition, there is the foot-falling
and implied cynicism in their use of the word "gratifies." Barnet, Berman and Burto seem to imply that there is something
of the impossible child in any reader "gratified" by the reading of that literature which they rightfully call "escapist."
Perhaps, after further consideration, Barnet, Berman, and
Burto would realize that that which they call "a never-never
land" is really more an "ever-ever land" since it would seem
rather ridiculous, if not frustrating, to "enter" what wasn't
there.

Implicit in the critical disdain of escape literature is a
journalistic ethic. Many critics and academic scholars continue to foster and protect a suspicious literary theory that encourages writers (if even in an oblique way) to account for
social and historical considerations. For such critics, the
purer expressions of language, such as Lewis Carroll's
"Alice's" have never been enough. Perhaps unwittingly, what
such critics say is that fiction and imagination are less acceptable as literary forms than as a derivative reportage. Escape
literature, especially the efforts of the benign humorists, promises little more than the next word, the next sentence, an
eventual back cover. It is, of course, all very literary.

Another critical approach that limits fair criticism of the late nineteenth- and twentieth-century writers of benign humor and escape literature is the curious form of critical relativism, already alluded to in a previous chapter. Such criticism assesses literature against like efforts of past epochs. The application of this perverse critical relativism has been especially unfortunate and unrewarding in terms of the literature of escape. The benign humorists cannot be extrapolated from their time and milieu, and to judge Milne against Addison, Grahame against Goldsmith or Sheridan is defeating and curiously uninformed. For the humorists of light literature, such critical loading would seem to be heavy and hard to bear. But where A. A. Milne never stopped reacting to such unfair criticism, P. G. Wodehouse takes the criticism and turns it deftly to his advantage. In *Performing Flea* he writes:

> A typical instance of the bad critic is the one who said, "it is time that Mr. Wodehouse realized that Jeeves has become a bore." When my press-cutting bureau sends me something like that, an icy-look comes into my hard grey eyes and I mark my displeasure by not pasting it in my scrapbook. Let us forget this type of man and turn to the rare souls who can spot a good thing when they see me, and shining like a beacon among them is the woman who wrote to the daily paper the other day to say that she considers Shakespeare "grossly materialistic and much overrated," and "greatly prefers P. G. Wodehouse."
>
> Well, it is not for me to say whether she is right or not. One cannot arbitrate in these matters of taste. Shakespeare's stuff is different than mine, but that is not necessarily to say that it is inferior. There are passages in Shakespeare to which I would have been quite pleased to put my name. That "tomorrow and tomorrow and tomorrow" thing. Some spin on the ball there. I doubt too, if I have ever done anything much better than Falstaff. The man may have been "grossly materialistic," but he would crack through the cover all right, when he got his eye in. I would definitely place him in the Wodehouse class.[176]

In an age of electronic media—a time where television dares the viewers not to watch—the critics of literature, sure that they are being attacked electronically, have come by their critical ambivalence quite naturally. The electronic media is more muscular than literature as it reports on contemporary ways of non-living. Indeed, television, almost single-handedly, has destroyed slick magazines such as *Life* and *Look*. Admittedly, the threat to print media is real. As a result, some critics and concerned academics have reacted in manners which have been more expressive than thoughtful. Assuming that they have a stake in opposing the electronic media, concerned literary critics tend to judge more generously the literature which fights the time. Unfortunately, the call for a more contemporaneous and more militant literature to combat the electronic media results in the viewing of late nineteenth- and twentieth-century humor and escape-literature in a way which seems to indicate that the electronic media was a force before and just after the turn of the century.

Television (that is the process of transmitting images to home screenings) seems, at first, to be merely the vehicle which has brought such literary classics as *War and Peace* and *The Forsyte Saga* to its viewing audience. At first, it seems an arrogant conceit to even attempt to adapt Tolstoy's *War and Peace* for television. But, in fact, television does not "adapt" so much as it reclassifies literary forms by forcing and materializing them into images which move graphically in front of a camera. Such an amendment of form does not speak to a literary fixity in type—a fixity which some "electronic theorists" incorrectly see as a lack of versatility and strength. Such criticism, however, is symptomatic of an "apple-orange" syndrome and offers little insight into theories of communication. But literary critics and academics must not confuse their criticism, for they should realize that television, if it attacks at all, attacks the medium of print and not the language and literature given birth and expression in print. It is equally clear that what is expressed in motion on film is, at some time before its being electronically activated, written on paper, i.e., script, scenario, stage directions, outlines, etc. In this regard, one wonders what Hall Bartlett's film *Jonathan Livingston Seagull* would have been without Richard Bach's prototypical work on gulling. Certainly, some theorists of modern, electronic media have offered delightful humors of their own. Typical of such puddling philosophies is a theory of Gene Youngblood (faculty member of California Institute of the Arts) who conditionally states that as the twentieth century "heats-up" and more and more young people are subjected to visual stimulation from films and television, people will *learn* to "think in the eye's retina."[178]

The benign humorists as well as other writers of escape literature such as Sayers and Conan Doyle, cared little for confrontation of any sort, be it with critics, traditions, or literative milieu. In fact, the benign humorists (with the exception of A. A. Milne) have always lived comfortably with balanced critical opinion. They were always quite happy to let their literature speak for them, even while the late nineteenth- and early twentieth-century wits stridently demanded that comic literature be more fairly recognized. Oscar Wilde, for example, was especially displeased at being labelled a raconteur and conversational wit. His answer to his critics was *The Ballad of Reading Gaol*.

The late nineteenth- and early twentieth-century critic and reader tended to dismiss the humorists and those of an escape *literati*, for people losing their innocence to politics and machines wanted literature -to *report* their problems. By the mid-twentieth century, however, people, always resourceful in time of stress, began to discover the literature of the benign humorists. By the middle of the twentieth century a small number of critics, most generously represented by John Aldridge, began to address the literature. There are even those academicians who boldly stock book stores with such "texts" as the *Annotated Alice*, the Pooh-stories, Grahame's *The Wind in the Willows*, and an occasional Wodehouse.

9.
Benign Humor and Escape:
A Prognosis

During the 1960s and the early 1970s, considerable research had been done, much of it admittedly unscientific and some of it merely bizarre, into the possible use of art forms for therapeutic means. One of the first "techniques" suggested by the energetic research is the use of music as a complement to the staple, therapy sessions. Simply stated, the research done by Bordinat's group of psychologists and graduate students has found music to be an effective way to unblock the communication between patient and therapist. More significant, if less sure, has been the group's research into the possible use of music as an alternative to certain pharmacological prescriptions. For example, Bordinat, after assessing the patient's therapeutic needs, will "prescribe" certain musics to meet the stated needs. The research has indicated that certain works of the more romantic composers such as Mahler, Debussy, and Brahms, if applied properly, does succeed in reducing anxiety and tension during and after traditional therapeutic sessions. In the same way, of course, Bordinat coyly recommends that the more melancholic patients undergoing experimentation listen to such stormy composers as Wagner and Beethoven.

More acceptable, perhaps, has been the recent research done in the area of potential uses of certain literatures for therapeutic means. The research, if relatively unsupported by any hard empirical data, has suggested promising, and humorous new ways to assess literature. Experimentation undertaken at Suffolk University in Boston, for example, suggests a therapeutic approach which com-

bines literature with certain bioenergetic exercises. The subject is asked to read (at home) key chapters and passages from selected literature while in various body positions. For example, one subject was asked to read the chapter entitled "Snow" from Thomas Mann's *Magic Mountain* while lying down, standing up, etc. On a subsequent visit to a psychologist's office, the subject who had been undergoing psychotherapy was asked to interpret the chapter "Snow" in terms of its effect while read in the various positions. As it turned out, the patient *enjoyed* the chapter most when she read it while standing up and walking about her house. If the approach seems somewhat unscientific, the conclusions of the psychologist are no less interesting. As a result of "testing" which utilizes Mann's *Magic Mountain,* the psychologist concluded that since lying down offers and implies comfort—comfort which detracts from therapeutic interaction—that the couch in her office was a "factor-of-comfort" which limited total concentration during the hour of analysis and congruent therapy. Similarly, the humanistic psychiatrist Henry E. Altenberg has found that therapeutic sessions of two hours or less can be rewarding and revealing if conducted with the therapist and patient on their feet and walking about. Indeed, movement stirs movement. In a more parochial sense, the psychologist concludes that reading of literature, at the very least, enables the patient "to fill in empty time which would have been otherwise filled with nervousness and anxiety."

Impressive research has also been undertaken in order to assess the effectiveness of literature as an alternative to drug therapy. The research tentatively indicates that literature can be used effectively as "direct medicine." Before using literature to mollify and alleviate nervous disorders, however, certain prerequisites must be met. First, the patient must demonstrate his or her "sensitivity to literature" in such a way that chances for an in-depth reading of the literature are virtually assured. Secondly, the therapist selects a bibliography which is prepared for each individual based on individual histories. Accordingly, patients are "prescribed" works of literature in such a way that the patient is convinced that the recommended works can and will substitute for the more scientifically ratified drugs. Such research, of course, is enhanced by its innate humor and good intentions.

There are difficult and almost insoluble problems attending the use of literature as a therapeutic tool. Not the least of the problems, of course, is the development of therapists who know literature well enough to "prescribe" it. It might even be recommended that since psychologists cannot legally prescribe drugs, that only Ph.D.'s in English be allowed to prescribe the appropriate literature.

Results of the research into the use of music and literature are still inconclusive and promise to remain so. The research, however, does suggest an awareness of extra-musical and extra-literary uses of art forms. Such approaches and techniques, however, be they "direct medicine" or therapeutic literature, seem too contrived and unscientific to be substantially successful in terms of other than personal therapy. The researchers who have studied the therapeutic uses of art are more likely to be successful if their research would begin to consider the subjective and purely selfish benefits of benign escape.

Final Note on Benign Humor as Literary Therapy

The nineteenth- and twentieth-century benign humorists and writers of escape literature continue to offer contemporary readers a literature of considerable artistry, endowed with an added dimension that had promised to remain dormant. By the 1960s, however, social unrest and cultural upheavings seemed to mitigate for the development of a new literature restricting fall-outs of *kitsch* and limiting the excesses of feverish journalists and quest-novelists. But writers in the years from 1960 to 1970 in America would only write about their troubles, and they left it to the historians to grieve; Philip Slater (*The Pursuit of Loneliness*) and others heard a discordant melody deep in the uneasy scan of the 1960s. The historians were similarly grieved.

By the late 1960s, however, American readers still indulged in quest-novels, sexual sociologies, mammarian novellas, and "how-to" primers which counseled sexual prowess and physical beauty no matter how costly. American readers saw institutions caught on the hooks of missed ethics and graft while political reputations fell like cake as political and social opinion leaders were something more and less than "good bricks." By the late 1960s, "mind-expanding" arts, "conscious-raising-isms," and the lowest common-denominatorism practiced by the electronic media became, for many, symptomatic of an ugly history processing its own scars. By the early 1970s, however, the literature of escape and benign humor reemerged as the works of the benign humorists rose without the bends from a deep sleep.

It is ironic that the benign humorists have been denied, not only fair criticism, but the compensations of popular success. The writers and academicians, however, are not totally to blame. It is a curious fact of literary life that the zealous but clubby readers of such humorists as Wodehouse, Milne, Grahame, as well as escape artists like Conan Doyle and Dorothy Sayers, have always fought attempts to draw attention to and thus popularize the literature. Such faithful readers seem to gather the books of the benign humorists like so many charmed cameos as they prefer to keep the literature still-born rather than share it with increasing numbers of new and what one Wodehousian calls "indiscreet readers." Many readers, some of them critics who wouldn't be caught dead admitting it, feel that the success of economic and even critical literature would threaten what a fan of Wodehouse calls "my corner on chiffon days and *souffle* nights." In the same way that many of Conan Doyle's readers resisted and resented the Sherlock Holmes films which starred Basil Rathbone and Nigel Bruce; P. G. Wodehouse's' readers remained suspicious and unconvinced as the two young English producers of the play *Jesus Christ Superstar* announced that their next production was to be *Jeeves: A Musical Comedy*. As one highly suspicious Wodehousian put it, "what can a twenty-year-old know about Plum Wodehouse?"

Many of the more tenured readers of the benign humorists rightfully worry the air over those who would distill the dreams of the literature in order to turn vapours into money. The future, however, bodes well for closeted fans of the humorists and escape *literati*. There is no reason to expect that those firm and growing mossy in front of television's unremitting eye and the youth who still opt for the amplified sweetmeats and wuzzes of rock universes will stampede the literature of the English humorists into some popular success.

The more possessive readers of the benign humorists feel they alone know what it is to carry bacon, slouch about in tooterbags, get locked-jawed on butter gams, wear checkered ties, sport madras hats and pin-striped pants. They alone are ready to admit to animals that have bowling leagues, and queue up at gas stations. A small readership always believed that the humorists have sociological information that knuts and animals have a taste for simple things such as onion sandwiches, coffee which perks and cradles in egg-shells, cooked newt, kippers with zippers, kidney sauce, asparagus pies, and brussel sprouts on melted ice cream. By the late 1960s, however, new appetites were being developed as those, addled by the times, were ready to believe anything, ready to embrace the humorists.

In the 1970s Sherlockian clubs are oversubscribed as pipes with dipped bowls and twin-peaked hats make consumer headway. Parents have heard the message as they buy Pooh-bears for their children, *whether the kids want them or not.* At the same time, bookstores are glutted with numerous editions of Grahame's *The Wind in the Willows,* and a plethora of Pooh-books including such curiosities as *The Pooh-Book for Sick People.* Television has not misjudged the new popularity of almost anything English; and the Public Broadcasting System's "Masterpiece Theater" continues to offer such "dramatizations" of Dorothy Sayer's Lord Peter Wimsey novels, as *Clouds of Witness, The Unpleasantness at the Bellona Club,* and *Murder Must Advertise.*

Clearly, by the late 1960s, and early 1970s, people young and old yearned for a "doo-dah" time which was neither bloodless nor Godless. The yearning for simpler times, however, could also dictate an appreciation for quicksilver popularity and simpleminded art. In terms of literature, people were gulled into making a sudden classic out of a story about a bird who seemed all enchantment, wisdom and ocean-spray, but who was, in reality like all other gulls—a supreme collector of garbage. Jonathan Livingston Seagull, in fact, seemed to pick up what he knew about Kahlil Gibran from Rod McKuen. The 1960's and 1970's reader was given a menu of tough cops, tough sex, and tough luck. The 1970's value system was strained somewhat as a Howard Cosell was loved for being hateful and the Jesuit priests Daniel and Phillip Berrigan smiled at summer flies on-the-bite, while, for some, the Berrigans became something just short of leftist bully-boys.

By the 1970s, however, some publishers, television executives, and magazine editors, saw, not only the opportunity to encourage the return to a more halcyon time, but, coincidentally, a chance to make money as well. They guessed correctly that Milne's Pooh-bear, who had been left sleeping in the 1950s and early 1960s, was just the animal to help young and old readers bear the times. Publishers stunned many who, in the 1970s, were surprised to hear that P. G. Wodehouse was still alive and *Jeeves and the Tie That Binds* was published by Simon and Schuster in 1972, while Kenneth Grahame's *The Wind in the Willows* remains stocked by most bookstores.

The sudden, if slight, popularity of the literature of the benign humorists as well as such writers of a more peripheral humor as Conan Doyle and Sayers, does not promise to dilute or inhibit an appreciation of the benign milieu by those readers who have always remained most faithful to it. There is no reason to suspect that new readers will diminish the criticism of many critics and literary scholars who lie in wait for something which they can turn to *kitsch*. The benign humorists, however, live safely in homes built in part from more recognized comic traditions but surrounded by the literature of purple trees, pink rivers, and substantial moats that are filled with sassy salmon and fringed by wing-tipped buttercups. The milieu of benign humor promises to endure even though P. G. Wodehouse alone remains to carry on the tradition. Benign literature will age

well and sustain itself, since it will be unhampered by the judg-
ments of time—time being something the humorists never recognize. It will also survive this book and others like it since
benign literature remains one of the few refuges for those people
crouched and pinched by the twentieth century, looking for
fine answers and new residence. Unfortunately, for some critics,
scholars, and wide numbers of readers, the cost of moving
is too exorbitant. Besides, what is the promise of smiles, laughs,
good will, and benign intent worth in terms of money, in terms
of perpetuating pessimism?

Notes

1. P. G. Wodehouse, *Ring for Jeeves* (London, Herbert Jenkins Limited, 1953), p. 72.

2. S. J. Perelman, *Acres and Pains* (New York: Simon and Schuster, 1972), pp. 58-59.

3. *English Wits,* ed. by Leonard Russell (London: Hutchinson, 1940), pp. viii-ix.

4. Walter Sorrel, *Facets of Comedy* (New York: Grosset Dunlap, 1972), p. 23.

5. George Vasey, *The Philosophy of Laughter and Smiling* (London: J. Burns, 1877), p. 169.

6. Stuart Tave, *The Amiable Humorist* (Chicago: Univ. of Chicago Press, 1960), pp. vii-viii.

7. Evan Esar, *The Humor of Humor* (New York: Horizon Press, 1952), pp. 13-33.

8. Stephen Leacock, *Humor and Humanity* (New York: Henry Holt and Co., 1938).

9. Ibid., p. 41.

10. Marshall McLuhan and Edmund Carpenter, "Acoustic Space," in *Explorations in Communication,* ed. by M. McLuhan and E. Carpenter (Boston: Beacon Press, 1960), pp. 65-70.

11. Leacock, *Humor and Humanity,* p. 169.

12. Gilbert Keith Chesterton, *A Handful of Authors* (New York: Sheed and Ward, 1953), p. 117.

13. George Orwell, *Shooting an Elephant* (London: Secker and Warburg, 1950), p. 183.

14. Walter Blair, *"A Man's Voice Speaking,"* in *Veins of Humor,* ed. by Harry Levin (Cambridge: Harvard Univ. Press, 1972), p. 188.

15. Edith Sitwell, *Horizon Magazine,* Winter 1972, p. 94.

16. Thomas L. Masson, *Our American Humorists* (Freeport, New York: Books for Libraries Press, Inc., 1931), p. 315.

17. Ibid., p. 315.

18. E. J. Oliver, *Hypocrisy and Humor* (New York: Sheed and Ward, 1960), p. 159.

19. J. B. Priestley, *English Humor* (London and New York: Longman's Green and Co. 1929), p. 5.

20. Ibid., p. 9.

21. William Somerset Maugham, *Cakes and Ale* (New York: P. F. Collier and Sons Corp., 1930), p. 26.

22. P. G. Wodehouse, *The Code of the Woosters* (New York: Doubleday, Doran and Co., 1939), p. 1.

23. Malcolm Bradbury, *The Social Context of Modern English Literature* (New York: Schocken Books, 1971).

24. Ibid., p. 57.

25. W. D. Hussey, *British History: 1815-1934* (Cambridge: University Press, 1968), p. 119.

26. R. J. Evans, *The Victorian Age: 1815-1914* (New York: St. Martins Press, 1968), p. iv.

27. William Thackeray, *English Humorists* (New York: Harper and Brothers, 1854), p. 282.

28. Ibid., p. 59.

29. John Timbs, *Lives of the Wits and Humorists* (London: Richard Bentley Co., 1862), p. 22.

30. Ibid., pp. 246-247.

31. R. G. G. Price, *A History of Punch* (London: Collins St. James Place, 1957), p. 46.

32. Ibid., p. 9.

33. Richard B. Ince, *Calverley and Some Cambridge Wits of the Nineteenth Century* (London: Grant Richards and Humphrey Toulmin, 1929), p. 11.

34. Ibid., p. 96.

35. Hesketh Pearson, *Lives of the Wits* (London, Melbourne, Toronto: Heinemann, 1962), p. 178.

36. Ibid., p. 197.

37. Ibid., p. 229.

38. Ibid., p. 293.

39. Ibid., p. 309.

40. Compton Mackenzie, *Literature in My Time* (New York: Loring and Mussey, 1933), pp. 73-83.

41. A. C. Ward, *The Nineteen-Twenties: Literature and Ideas in the Post-War Decade* (London: Methuen and Co. Ltd., 1930), p. 120.

42. Stuart Tave, *The Amiable Humorist* (Chicago: Univ. of Chicago Press, 1960), p. 187.

43. A. C. Ward, *The Nineteen-Twenties: Literature and Ideas in the Post-War Decade* p. 187.

44. A. A. Milne, *By Way of Introduction* (London: Methuen and Co., 1929), p. 193.

45. Ivar Brown, *J. B. Priestley* (London: Longmans Green and Co., 1957), p. 16.

46. Patricia Meyers Spacks, "Logic and Language in 'Through the Looking-Glass,'" *Aspects of Alice: Lewis Carroll's Dreamchild As Seen Through the Critics Looking-Glasses,* ed. by Robert Phillips (New York: The Vanguard Press, Inc. 1971), p. 268.

47. Elizabeth Sewell, "The Balance of Brillig," *The Field of Nonsense* (London: Chatto and Windus Ltd., 1952), p. 129.

48. Elizabeth Sewell, "Lewis Carroll and T. S. Eliot as Nonsense Poets," *Aspects of Alice* pp. 119-260.

49. John Ciardi, "A Burble through the Tulgey Wood," *Aspects of Alice* p. 27.

50. Lewis Carroll, *Alice in Wonderland* (London: Collier-Macmillan Ltd. 1962), p. 27.

51. Ibid., p. 28.

52. Ibid., p. 92.

53. Ibid., p. 113.

54. Walter Sorrel, *Facets of Comedy* (New York: Grosset Dunlap, 1972).

55. Elizabeth Sewell, *The Field of Nonsense* (London: Chatto and Windus, 1952), pp. 25-26.

56. Edward Lear, *Teapots and Quails,* ed. by Angus Davidson and Phillip Hofer (Cambridge: Harvard Univ. Press, 1953), p. 16.

57. Ibid., p. 20.

58. Ibid., p. 21.

59. Ibid., p. 24.

60. Ibid., p. 25.

61. Ibid., p. 27.

62. Ibid., p. 29.

63. Ibid., p. 32.

64. Ibid., p. 31.

65. Ibid., p. 34.

66. Ibid., p. 37.

67. Ibid., p. 45.

68. Ibid., p. 47.

69. Ibid., p. 48.

70. William Blake, "Infant Joy," in *Blake* with an Introduction by Ruthuen Todd (New York: Dell Publishing Co., 1960), p. 50.

71. Thomas Burnett Swann, *A. A. Milne* (New York: Twayne Publishers, 1971), p. 93.

72. Ibid., p. 130.

73. A. A. Milne, *Winnie the Pooh* in *The World of Pooh* (New York: E. P. Dutton and Co., Inc., 1957), p. 136.

74. Ibid., pp. 9-10.

75. Ibid., p. 27.

76. Ibid., p. 114.

77. Ibid., p. 15.

78. Ibid., p. 30.

79. Ibid., p. 41.

80. Ibid., p. 38.

81. Ibid., p. 46.

82. Ibid., pp. 50-53.

83. Ibid., p. 39.

84. Ibid., p. 76.

85. Ibid., pp. 82-83.

86. Ibid., pp. 103-104.

87. Ibid., pp. 103-104.

88. Ibid., p. 122.

89. A. A. Milne, *The House at Pooh Corner* in *The World of Pooh* (New York: E. P. Dutton and Co., Inc., 1957), p. 157.

90. Ibid., p. 160.

91. Ibid., p. 244.

92. Ibid., p. 285.

93. Ibid., p. 183.
94. Ibid., p. 178.
95. Ibid., p. 180.
96. Ibid., p. 181.
97. Ibid., p. 254.
98. Ibid., pp. 270-271.
99. Ibid., p. 307.
100. Ibid., p. 216.
101. Margaret Lane, *The Tale of Beatrix Potter* (London and New York: Frederick Warne and Co. Ltd., 1946), p. 116.
102. Ibid., p. 118.
103. May Hill Arbuthnot, *Children and Books* (Chicago: Scott, Foresman and Co., 1964), p. 348.
104. Richard Voohees, *P. G. Wodehouse* (New York: Twayne Publishers Inc., 1966), p. 162.
105. Richard Usborne, *Wodehouse at Work* (London: Herbert Jenkins Limited, 1961), p. 193.
106. R. B. D. French, *P. G. Wodehouse* (London: Oliver Boyd, 1966), p. 73.
107. Richard Usborne, *Wodehouse at Work*, pp. 195-210.
108. P. G. Wodehouse, *Very Good Jeeves* (London: Herbert Jenkins Limited, 1930), p. 309.
109. Richard Usborne, *Wodehouse at Work*, pp. 195-210.
110. P. G. Wodehouse, *Very Good Jeeves*, p. 309.
111. P. G. Wodehouse and W. H. Townend, *Author, Author* (New York: Simon and Schuster, 1962), p. 16.
112. Peter Green, *Kenneth Grahame* (Cleveland and New York: World Publishing Co., 1959).
113. May Hill Arbuthnot, *Children and Books* (Chicago: Scott, Foresman and Co., 1964), pp. 348-351.
114. Kenneth Grahame, *The Wind in the Willows* (New York: The Heritage Press, 1956), pp. 106-107.
115. Ibid., pp. 50-51.
116. Ibid., pp. 43-44.
117. Ibid., p. 64.
118. Ibid., p. 119.
119. Ibid., p. 121.
120. Ibid., p. 129.
121. Ibid., p. 130.
122. Ibid., p. 93.
123. Ibid., p. 9.
124. Ibid., p. 58.
125. Ibid., p. 54.
126. Ibid., p. 54.
127. Ibid., p. 56.
128. Ibid., p. 72.
129. Doris Ross McCrosson, *Walter de la Mare* (New York: Twayne Publishers, 1966), p. 49.
130. Ibid., p. 68.
131. Ibid., p. 71.
132. Ibid., pp. 18-20.

133. Forest Reid, *Walter de la Mare: A Critical Study* (London: Faber and Faber, 1929), p. 185.

134. Henry Charles Duffin, *Walter de la Mare: A Study of His Poetry* (London: Sidgwick and Jackson Limited, 1949), p. 58-60.

135. Ibid., pp. 150-151.

136. Ibid., pp. 155-156.

137. Ibid., p. 198.

138. Walter de la Mare, "Lovelocks," *Songs of Childhood* (1902) in *The Complete Poems*, p. 4.

139. Ibid., "Tartary," p. 5.

140. Ibid., p. 5.

141. Ibid., "Down-a-down Derry." p. 29.

142. Walter de la Mare, "The Huntsmen," *Peacock Pie* (New York: Henry Holt and Co., n.d.), p. 39.

143. Walter de la Mare, "The Mulgar's Farewell," *The Three Royal Monkeys* (1910) in *The Complete Poems of Walter de la Mare* (New York: Alfred A. Knopf, 1970), p. 727.

144. Walter de la Mare, "Andy's Battle Song," in *Crossings: A Fairy Play* (1921) in *The Complete Poems*, p. 729.

145. Walter de la Mare, "The Bandog," *Peacock Pie* (New York: Henry Holt and Co., n.d.), p. 11.

146. Walter de la Mare, "Captain Lean" in *Songs of Childhood* (1902) in *The Complete Poems*, p. 39.

147. Walter de la Mare, "The Apple Charm" in *Poems for Children* (1930), in *The Complete Poems*, p. 266.

148. Walter de la Mare, "There Sate Good Queen Bess," in *Crossings: A Fairy Play* (1921), in *The Complete Poems*, p. 739.

149. Walter de la Mare, "The Tulips" in *Stuff and Nonsense* (1927) in *The Complete Poems*, p. 844.

150. Ibid., "The Duet," p. 845.

151. Walter de la Mare, "Puss" in *Poems for Children* (1930) in *The Complete Poems*, p. 268.

152. Walter de la Mare, "Fol, dol, Do," in *Crossings: A Fairy Play* (1921) in *The Complete Poems* p. 714.

153. Walter de la Mare, "Sam Lover" in *Ding Dong Bell* (1924) in *The Complete Poems*, p. 750.

154. Walter de la Mare, "The Mouse" in *Stuff and Nonsense*, in *The Complete Poems*, p. 843.

155. *McLuhan Hot and Cool*, ed. by Gerald Emmanuel Stearn (New York: The Dial Press, 1967), p. 268.

156. William P. Alston, *Philosophy of Language* (Englewood Cliffs: Prentice Hall, Inc., 1964), p. 96.

157. I. A. Richards, "The Interaction of Words" in *The Language of Poetry* ed. by Allan Tate (New York: Russel and Russel, 1960), p. 71.

158. W. K. Wimsatt, *The Verbal Icon* (Lexington: University of Kentucky Press, 1954), p. 198-217.

159. Louis MacNeice, *Modern Poetry: A Personal Essay* (London: Oxford University Press, 1938), pp. 160-161.

160. P. G. Wodehouse, "Jeeves and the Indian Summer of an Uncle," in *Very Good Jeeves* (London: Herbert Jenkins Limited, 1930), p. 274.

161. P. G. Wodehouse, *The Code of the Woosters* (London: Herbert Jenkins Limited, 1962), p. 7.

162. Benjamin Lee Whorf, *Language, Thought and Reality* ed. by John B. Carroll (Cambridge: M.I.T. Press, 1970), p. 248.

163. Kenneth Grahame, *The Wind in the Willows* (New York: The Heritage Press, 1940), p. 8.

164. A. A. Milne, *Winnie the Pooh* in *The World of Pooh* (New York: E. P. Dutton and Co., 1957), p. 20.

165. Frederick C. Crews, *The Pooh Perplex* (New York: E. P. Dutton and Co., Co., 1963), pp. 75-85.

166. A. A. Milne, *Winnie the Pooh*, p. 28.

167. David Daiches, *English Literature* (Englewood Cliffs New Jersey: Prentice Hall, Inc., 1964), p. 99.

168. Kenneth Grahame, *The Wind in the Willows* (New York: The Heritage Press, 1940), p. 98.

169. George Steiner, "In A Post Culture," *Extraterritorial Papers on Literature and the Language of Revolution* (New York: Atheneum, 1971), pp. 155-171.

170. P. G. Wodehouse, *Performing Flea: A Self Portrait in Letters* (London: Herbert Jenkins Limited, 1953), p. 31.

171. Arthur Conan Doyle, "A Scandal in Bohemia," in *The Complete Sherlock Holmes* (New York: Doubleday and Co., n.d.), p. 161.

172. Richard Usborne, *Wodehouse at Work* (London: Herbert Jenkins Limited, 1961), p. 153.

173. R. B. D. French, *P. G. Wodehouse* (London: Oliver Boyd, 1966), p. 107.

174. Dorothy Sayers, *Lord Peter* with an Introduction by James Sandoe (New York: Avon Books, 1972), p. xii.

175. Sylvan Barnet, Morton Berman, William Burto, *The Study of Literature* (Boston: Little Brown and Co., 1960), p. 297.

176. P. G. Wodehouse, *Performing Flea: A Self Portrait In Letters*, p. 59.

177. Gene Youngblood, *Show Magazine,* Summer 1970.

Appendix

During a one-year period from 1972-1973, a group of graduate students, studying for their masters degree in English literature, underwent extensive testing in order to determine the feasibility of using literature as a "therapeutic tool." The testing was administered by a psychologist and a professor of communication research and was undertaken in order to specifically tap the escape potential inherent in the literature of those writers called benign-humorists.

The testing, although highly theoretical and extremely speculative, has revealed, at the very least, new ways to speculate about literature. The subsequent experimentation, which "used" the Milne books, *Winnie the Pooh* and *The House at Pooh Corner,* Kenneth Grahame's *The Wind in the Willows* as well as Lewis Carroll's *Alice in Wonderland,* also indicates the lengths to which theorists will extend insights based on charmed readings.

It is not particularly germane or even helpful to outline the criteria used to select the test group except to indicate that the group was selected from volunteers who indicated a favorable predisposition toward the "test literature" as well as indicating their belief in the general thesis of escape.

According to those administering the "testing," certain guidelines must be recognized before "favorable testing" is commenced. They are,

137

1. A simply stated desire, or an occasionally felt need, to "escape." A desire which could be simply indicated by such expressions as "I've got to get away from it all," etc.

2. An understanding and an appreciation of the literature of the benign-humorists which could give the reader the *information* and *feel* necessary to question and, hopefully, dismiss such preconditioned responses to the literature of the humorists as:

   a. "children's literature is just for kids."

   b. "nonsense literature, such as that written by Carroll and Lear, is an indication of a lack of 'literary seriousness.'"

   c. "To 'escape' from something or someone is, somehow, a sign of immaturity and insecurity."

First results of the testing show that it is necessary to simulate a "congenial reading environment" in which the literature of the humorists can, hopefully, be read for reasons of extra-literary escape. The room subsequently chosen for the *testing* of Milne's *Winnie the Pooh* was located in a private residence in the quiet town of Canton, Connecticut. The room was chosen for its country location as well as for its material properties which could be amended and altered quickly. Preliminary results showed that if the people being tested were overly conscious of their environment, the surroundings tended to intrude on the reading process, thereby defeating the chances for total immersion, for escape in the literature. Before testing was begun, the room was altered so that all obstacles to reader concentration were neutralized. It was subsequently found that "too much noise" or "too little noise" were equally disruptive. (Illustrating the disruptive quality of "too little noise" is the experience of composer John Cage. Cage, while looking for a "totally sound-proof environment," was "introduced" to a Harvard Physics Laboratory which had been apparently converted into a sound-proof environment called an "aechoic chamber." Once inside the "aechoic chamber," however, Cage reported hearing a "high sound" and a "distinctly low sound." Upon emerging from the room, Cage was told that the high sound he heard was the sound of his nervous system, while the low sound he had alluded to was merely the circulation of his blood.) The testing room, therefore, was chosen in such a way that "natural noises" (birds, cars, etc.) were not excluded from the room.

The room selected for the readings was further altered in a way which promised to make the reading process more "congenial." For the readings of Milne's Pooh-stories, the original room's abstract lithographs, cubist prints and serigraphs were taken from the walls and replaced with brightly-colored prints depicting what one reader called "bucolic and pastoral settings." In addition, a red and white checkered throw was placed over the room's rather "somber appearing couch." Attached to two heat-vents in the room's ceiling was a string of five bells which chimed whenever heat was forced through the vents. The room's telephone was disconnected and its book shelves were replenished with volumes of such so called "children's literature" as Beatrix Potter's animal books and E. B. White's Stuart Little stories. Wary of "over-contriving" the room's environment, a stereo record player was supplied on which the reader being tested could play "supplemental music" of his choosing.

Once familiar with the room and properly disposed toward "using" literature for extra-literary purposes, the students were asked to read A. A. Milne's *Winnie the Pooh*—a reading which took approximately one and a half to two hours. To determine the successful "immersion" of the reader "into the literature"—the *escape* itself—key questions were asked immediately following the reading. One woman who was considered a "successful test" was asked:

Q: Did you enjoy the book?
A: Yes, it was great.
Q: Did you enjoy E. H. Shepard's illustrations? Did they add to your enjoyment of the story?
A: Yes, they were fantastic but I wouldn't say they added anything. They just sort of showed how Milne wanted his animals to look.
Q: Which of the story's characters did you find most attractive in terms of behavior, personality, likeability, etc.?
A: Uh, well . . . I guess Pooh and Christopher Robin, but I really liked them all.

Q: What did you think of the way Pooh and the other animals
made fun of Eeyore?
A: They did?

Among the more curious conclusions drawn by those administering the text are the following:

1. The reader expressed her obvious pleasure with the book
which, in turn, indicated both her ability to read the story meaning-
fully and her enthusiam for the story itself.

2. The reader indicated that Shepard's illustrations, although
pleasing, and, perhaps, helpful, were not equally as significant as
the story itself. We conclude that the "immersion into" the literature itself was rather complete in that the reader was not de-
flected from the language by accompanying visuals and graphics.

3. The reader apparently saw all the characters in the story as
attractive and likeable. This attested to the literature's escape
potential in that the reader, once intoxicated by the likeability
of Christopher Robin, Pooh, *et al.,* tended not to see Owl's,
Eeyore's and Tigger's less attractive traits.

4. The reader was *not* conscious of Pooh, or anyone else for
that matter, making fun of the donkey Eeyore. There seems in the
mind of this successful test not even the remotest hint of acri-
monious behavior and ill-wishes.

It would be inappropriate for me to comment on the reasons for
the testing, its methodology or, for that matter, the encouragement
those administering the test received from a study I had done in
1971 on the subject of benign-literature. It is appropriate, however,
to offer a few comments.

It is apparent that the literature of the benign-humorists and
the more designed escapes of Conan Doyle and Dorothy Sayers can
be utilized in ways which all *individual* readers to escape in the
sense of filling time *expected* with an alternative time which is,
in fact, timeless and stress-free. The concept of individual escape
is, perhaps, the most realizable literary escape.

Research, testing and therapeutic application, although interesting
and intellectually energetic, seems destined to fulfill one one of

the well-intentioned definitions of "humor." Such testing and resultant therapeutic device overexamines and overuses a literature
which, if it is to be enjoyed as escape at all, must be left alone
and free of the more pedantic and modish theorists who would adapt
the literature for those *direct* therapeutic purposes which, after
all, run counter to the stated and implied wishes of the benign-
humorists.

Indeed, direct and quasi-scientific use of the literature of the
benign-humorists is not indicated at this time, and would be
doomed to what theorists might call "direct failure." The literature of the humorists, however, is a literary self-therapy. The
literature offers all the charm of escape without the imminent
threat of introspective questionings. The benign-literature of the
humorists can be read—thus used— in a personal, private way which
is, in fact, the only true way to a literary escape of any significance.
Indeed, the literature of the benign-humorists is highly recommended for those most in need of such an escape and attendant
therapy—those very same critics who continue to deny the worth
and literary value of the literature.

Bibliographical Notes

Chapter 1

Of great assistance when assessing the essential differences between the nineteenth and twentieth century wits and humorists are *English Wits* (London, 1946) edited by Leonard Russel, *Veins of Humor* (Cambridge, 1972) edited by Harry Levin, and the late-nineteenth century effort by F. R. Fleet, *A Theory of Wit and Humor* (London, 1890).

Useful in helping to establish the incongruent English and American senses of humor are *The Philosophy of Laughter and Smiling* (London, 1877) by George Vasey, *Psychology of Laughter* (New York, 1919) by Boris Sidis, *Humor and Humanity* (New York, 1938) by Stephen Leacock, *The Humor of Humor* (New York, 1952) by Evan Esar, *The Sense of Humor* (New York, 1921) by Max Eastman and *The Rise and Fall of American Humor* (New York, 1968) by Jesse Bier.

Helpful in a curious and supplemental sense is *English Satire and Satirists* (New York, 1925) written by Hugh Walker, and George Orwell's *Shooting an Elephant* (London, 1950).

When assessing the differences and nuances which attend the respective literary traditions extant in both nineteenth and twentieth century America and England, the following texts should be consulted: *English Humor* (London, 1929) by J. B. Priestley, *The*

Amiable Humorist (Chicago, 1960) by Stuart Tave, Thomas Masson's *Our American Humorists* (New York, 1931), *Facets of Comedy* (New York, 1972) by Walter Sorrel, *Hypocrisy and Humor* (New York, 1960) by E. J. Oliver and *The American Humorist: Conscience of the Twentieth Century* (Ames, Iowa, 1964) by Norris W. Yates.

In a secondary sense, the essay "Acoustic Space" by Marshall McLuhan and Edmund Carpenter and Edith Sitwell's comments on *English Eccentrics* (Horizon Magazine, Winter 1972) were helpful. In addition, William Somerset Maugham's *Cakes and Ale* (New York, 1930) offers an oblique but no less helpful insight into an Englishman's apprehension of the American sense of humor.

In addition to the major wits and humorists mentioned in the text, it is helpful to read the works of secondary writers of humor and wit including Sydney Smith, Francis Hutcheson, John Gay and the rather whimsical offerings of journalist Thomas De Quincey. The wits and humorists of *Punch* should not be overlooked. Of special interest are the illustrators John Leech and Charles Keene, as well as the urbane witticisms of Shirley Brooks. Other significant writers for *Punch* include Albert Smith ("Physiologies"), Francis Burnaud (inventor of a "spoof-journalism") and E. J. Milliken who wrote comic verses about the cockney bounder, "Arry."

Chapter 2

When tracing the roots of the comic tradition in English literature, a discussion of social *milieu* and cultural context is necessary. Helpful in this sense are *British History: 1815-1934* (Cambridge, 1968) by W. D. Hussey, *The Victorian Age: 1815-1914* (New York, 1968) by R. J. Evans and *A History of Punch* (London, 1957) written by R. G. G. Price. Of a secondary importance are *The Nineteen-Twenties: Literature and Ideas in a Post-War Decade* (London, 1930) by A. C. Ward, *Literature in My Time* (New York,

1933) by Compton Mackenzie, *The Social Context of Modern English Literature* (New York, 1971) by Malcolm Bradbury, *The Georgian Scene* (London, 1951) by Frank Swinnerton and John Fyvie's *Wits, Beaux and Beauties of the Georgian Era* (London, 1909).

To further distinguish the significant differences between wit, satire and humor, the following books are invaluable: *Calverley and Some Cambridge Wits of the Nineteenth Century* (London, 1929) by Richard B. Ince, *Lives of the Wits* (London, Melbourne, Toronto, 1962) by Hesketh Pearson, *English Humorists* (New York, 1854) written by William Thackeray and *The Lives of the Wits and Humorists* (London, 1862) by John Timbs. Supplementing the preceding texts are *Dickens, Dali and Others* (New York, 1946) by George Orwell, *The Satiric Art of Evelyn Waugh* (Seattle, 1966) by James F. Carens, G. K. Chesterton's *A Handful of Authors* (New York, 1953), *The Age of Extravagance* (New York, 1954) edited by Mary Elisabeth Edes and Dudley Frasier and *Essays and Reflections* (Cambridge, 1948) by Harold Child.

Contributing to the chapter were comments from *By Way of Introduction* (London, 1929) by A. A. Milne, *J. B. Priestley* (London, 1957) by Ivor Brown and, curiously enough, Malcolm Cowley's *Exiles Return* (New York, 1934).

Chapter 3

In addition to primary readings of the benign-humorists, especially *Teapots and Quails* (Cambridge, 1953) Edward Lear's work edited by Angus Davidson and Phillip Hofer, and Lewis Carroll's *Alice in Wonderland* and *Through the Looking-Glass* (London, 1962), *Facets of Comedy* (New York, 1972) by Walter Sorrel and *The Field of Nonsense* (London, 1952) by Elizabeth Sewell are indispensable. (The latter work is the quintessential statement of nonsense language and literature.)

When addressing the literature of Lewis Carroll, Robert Phillips's edition *Aspects of Alice: Lewis Carroll's Dreamchild As Seen Through the Critic's Looking-Glasses* (New York, 1971) is necessary reading.

Especially significant essays from the Phillips text are "Logic and Language in *Through the Looking-Glass*" by Patricia Meyers Spacks, "The Poems in *Alice in Wonderland*" by Florence Milner, "Lewis Carroll and T. S. Eliot as Nonsense Poets" by Elizabeth Sewell and John Ciardi's "A Burble Through the Tulgey Wood."

Of added importance are "What is A Boojum? Nonsense and Modernism" by Michael Holquist (New York, n.d.) and Donald Rackin's essay "Alice's Journey to the Edge of Night" (New York, n.d.).

Chapter 4

There is no critical substitute for a highly subjective reading and interpretation of the prototypical works of benign-humor of "children's literature," A. A. Milne's *Winnie the Pooh* and *The House at Pooh Corner* (New York, 1957), P. G. Wodehouse's Bertie Wooster and Jeeves short stories and novels and Beatrix Potter's animal tales, especially *Peter Rabbit, Squirrel Nutkin, Jemima Puddle Duck* and *The Tailor of Gloucester*.

Critical looks at the literature are offered by *A. A. Milne* (New York, 1971) by Thomas Burnett Swann, *The Tale of Beatrix Potter* (London, New York, 1946) by Margaret Lane, *Wodehouse at Work* (London, 1961) by Richard Usborne, *P. G. Wodehouse* (London, 1966) by R. B. D. French and *P. G. Wodehouse* (New York, 1966) written by Richard Voorhees.

Also of assistance is May Hill Arbuthnot's *Children and Books* (Chicago, 1964), *Wooster's World* (London, 1967) by

Geoffrey Jaggard, *The World of P. G. Wodehouse* (New York, 1972) by Herbert Warren Wind, *The Comic Style of P. G. Wodehouse* (Hamden, Conn., 1974) by Robert A. Hall Jr., the essay "The Lesson of the Young Master," John Aldridge's introduction to *Selected Stories of P. G. Wodehouse* (New York, 1958), and "The Antecedents of P. G. Wodehouse" in *Arizona Quarterly* (Autumn, 1949) written by Lionel Stevenson.

Chapter 5

The specific works discussed in the chapter are *The Wind In The Willows* (New York, 1956) by Kenneth Grahame, Walter de la Mare's collected works *Songs of Childhood* (London, 1902), *Peacock Pie* (London, 1913), *The Three Royal Monkeys* (London, 1910), *Crossings: A Fairy Play* (London, 1921), *Poems for Children* (London, 1930), *Stuff and Nonsense* (London, 1927) and *Ding Dong Bell* (London, 1930).

The more significant critiques of the work of Kenneth Grahame and Walter de la Mare include *Kenneth Grahame* (Cleveland and New York, 1959) by Peter Green, *Kenneth Grahame* (New York, 1963) by Eleanor Grahame, *Walter de la Mare: A Critical Study* (London, 1929) by Forest Reid, *Walter de la Mare: A Study of His Poetry* (London, 1949) by Henry Charles Duffin and *Walter de la Mare* (New York, 1966) written by Doris Ross McCrosson.

Chapter 6

In addition to reading the works of the benign-humorists, it is necessary to establish fundamentally new ways to read and assess the language of the humorists.

Before deciding on methodological approaches to the literature, however, it is helpful to read *Language, Thought and Reality* (Cambridge, 1970) and other writings of Benjamin Lee Whorf, *The Philosophy of Language* (New Jersey, 1964) by William P. Alston and *The Language of Poetry* edited by Allan Tate (New York, 1960). An especially significant essay in Tate's book is "The Interaction of Words" by I. A. Richards.

Of a less significant nature is *The Verbal Icon* (Lexington, 1954) by W. K. Wimsatt and Monroe Beardsley, and *Modern Poetry: A Personal Essay* (London, 1938) by Louis MacNeice. In a more whimsical vein, of course, is *McLuhan Hot and Cool* (New York, 1967) edited by Gerald Emmanuel Stearn. More patronizing is the delightful *The Pooh Perplex* (New York, 1963) written by Frederick C. Crews.

In addition to Milne's Pooh-stories and Kenneth Grahame's *The Wind in the Willows,* especially germane to a discussion of the language of the benign-humorists are P. G. Wodehouse's *The Code of the Woosters* (London, 1962), and the collection *Very Good Jeeves* (London, 1930).

Also of interest is Gilbert Ryle's essay "Systematically Misleading Expressions" (1931-1932) which appears in *An Introduction to Philosophical Inquiry* (New York, 1968) edited by Joseph Margolis.

Also recommended are *The Art of James Thurber* (Athens Ohio, 1969) by Richard C. Tobias and, for a general sampling of the language of the late nineteenth and early twentieth century humorists, *An Outline of Humor* (London, 1932) edited by Carolyn Wells. A supplemental and intriguing book is *Here, There and Everywhere* (London, 1932) by Eric Partridge.

Chapter 7

When discussing the literature and language of the benign-humorists in order to determine its escape potential, it is important that analyses and consequential results be originally undertaken and subjectively applied. With this in mind, useful secondary sources are at a minimum and not recommended.

In a limited sense, however, the following books are helpful, *English Literature* (Englewood Cliffs, 1964) by David Daiches and *Extraterritorial: Papers on Literature and the Language of Revolution* (New York, 1971) by George Steiner.

Chapter 8

Significant material when assessing the appropriateness of critical opinion which directly, and more often than not, indirectly attends the literature of the benign-humorists and other writers of escape is offered in *The Study of Literature* (Boston, 1960) by Sylvan Barnet, Morton Berman and William Burto and in *An Essay on Criticism* (New York, 1966) by Graham Hough. Other critical works considered in the chapter are Usborne's *Wodehouse at Work* (London, 1961) and *P. G. Wodehouse* (London, 1966) by R. B. D. French.

Of additional interest are James Sandoe's introduction to *Lord Peter* (New York, 1972) by Dorothy Sayers and Wodehouse's rather unrevealing *Performing Flea: A Self Portrait in Letters* (London, 1953).

Especially helpful when drawing the appropriate comparisons between Wodehouse's literary team of Bertie Wooster and Jeeves and Conan Doyle's literary team of Sherlock Holmes and Doctor Watson, is Conan Doyle's "A Scandal in Bohemia" which appears in *The Complete Sherlock Holmes* (New York, n.d.).

In addition to the literature of the humorists mentioned in the text, the primary readings recommended for a proper assessment of escape literature include Dorothy Sayers's *Clouds of Witness* (New York, 1926) *The Unpleasantness at the Bellona Club* (New York, 1928) and *The Five Red Herrings* (New York, 1931). Recommended readings of Conan Doyle should include, *The Speckled Band* (London, 1912) and *The Adventure of the Blue Carbuncle* (New York, 1948).

Chapter 9

Of particular interest when considering the element of escape in literature is A. A. Alvarez's *The Savage God* (New York, 1972).

Of minor importance is Philip Slater's *The Pursuit of Loneliness* (Boston, 1970).

Index

151

ritorial expression in literature of, 70; "Down-adown-Derry," 72-73; "Lovelocks," 72; "The Huntsman," 73; "Tartary," 73; "Andy's Battle Song," 74; "The Bandog," 74; "Apple Charm," 75; "Captain Lean," 75; "The Duet," 76; "There Sate Good Queen Bess," 76; "Fol, Dol, Do," 77; "Puss," 77
Dickens, Charles, 28, 44, 113
Disraeli, Benjamin, 19
Douglas, Lord Alfred, *The Spirit Lamp,* 26
Doyle, Arthur Conan, 111-115; comparison to Wodehouse, 112-115; 112-113; escapist dimensions of literature, 112-113; comparison to literature of Dorothy Sayers, 115-118; "The Adventure of the Devil's Foot," 116; "The Adventure of the Engineer's Thumb," 116; "The Adventure of the Red Carbuncle," 116; "The Adventure of the Speckled Band," 113; Holmes as diagnostician, 117; closed readership of, 127-128; literary clubs, 128
Drones Clubs, 59, 89, 102
Dryden, John, 4
Dunsany, Lord, *The Tortoise and the Hare,* 30

Eastman, Max, 5, 6
Electronic Media, 121-123, print media, 122; adaptation of print matter, 122-123; 128-129
Ellis, H. F., 29
England, 16; intellectual climate in, 16-19; view of materialism, 18-19; concept of individualism, 19; Victorian England, 19-20; Industrial Revolution in, 28, 29
Escape, 3, 93-110; concept of destination, 94, 105-110; instinctual base of, 96; concept of route, 98-

99; concept in literature of Milne, Grahame and Wodehouse, 98-102; anti-metaphorical base of, 102-103, 106; concept of in the literature of Sayers and Conan Doyle, 115-118; therapeutic use, 124-130

Fielding, Henry, 20
Fitzgerald, Edward, 23

Garstin, Crosbie, 29
Gay, John, 20
Gilbert, William S., *The Palace of Truth,* 24; *The Wicked World,* 24; compared to Wodehouse, 58
Golsmith, Oliver, 20-21, 121
Gladstone, William, 19
Grahame, Harry, 29
Grahame, Kenneth, 15, 29-30; 63-68; as literary "fabulist," 63; *The Wind in the Willows,* 63; Homeric interpretation, 64, 91; element of terror in literature, 65; religious themes in *The Wind in the Willows,* 66; miniature literary worlds, 67, 83; view of "absurdist literature," 67; 83; class structure in *The Wind in the Willows,* 67-68; dimensions of language, 87-92; pantheism in *The Wind in the Willows,* 88-89; euphonic use, 99-100
Guthrie, Thomas A., *Three Men in a Boat,* 30; *Vice-Versa,* 30

Hazlitt, William, 4
Hogarth, William, 20
Hook, Theodore, 28
Humor, 1-3; distinction between wit and humor, 3-6; classifications of, 4-9; American and English distinctions, 5; Satire, 5, 8; "Humorology," 8; English and American senses of, 9-12; roots